LET'S Celebrate

A Low-Carb Cookbook for Year-Round Entertaining

BESTSELLING AUTHOR OF *SOUTHERN KETO*
NATASHA NEWTON

VICTORY BELT PUBLISHING
Las Vegas

To Chris. I'm so thankful we've been given more time to celebrate life together. I love you!

Cover and back cover photos by Justin-Aaron Velasco and Kat Lannom

Food styling for cover and back cover photos by Marcella Capasso

Recipe photos by Natasha Newton

Author and tablescape photography by Erika Bentley, Evolve Creative

Tablescape design and styling by Rachael Wofford, MW Events

Makeup by Taylor Newton

Interior design and illustrations by Justin-Aaron Velasco and Kat Lannom

Printed in Canada

TC 0123

CONTENTS

INTRODUCTION

Welcome back, y'all! I'm so excited to bring you my third cookbook, *Let's Celebrate: A Low-Carb Cookbook for Year-Round Entertaining.* It was such a joy to write my first two books, and I was honored to see so many of my recipes become your family favorites. Your support means the world to me and continues to inspire me to create simple and comforting low-carb recipes with Southern flair.

So much has transpired in our world since *Southern Keto* was published in 2018. My second book, *Southern Keto: Beyond the Basics,* was released in the early days of the Covid-19 pandemic. During that time, I was feeling closed off from family and friends as our gatherings were put on hold. I missed their company and the carefree way of life we were used to. With restrictions starting to be lifted, the idea for this book was born. We've come a long way, and it has me in a celebratory mood!

Beginning to plan this book got me thinking about what it truly means to gather. I used to think only large-scale get-togethers qualified as celebrations, but for two-plus years, many of us celebrated holidays, birthdays, anniversaries, and other special occasions with very few people in attendance. Still, we celebrated! Even more importantly, we learned to celebrate life's smallest moments.

I believe in living each day as though it were your last. Having recently faced many obstacles of my own, I've come to appreciate the little things more than ever. My husband endured a life-threatening injury while I was writing this book. It was a terrifying time for our family, though thankfully he has recovered. In a lot of ways, it was an eye-opening experience—another reason why I feel thankful and intend to celebrate life each and every day!

Let's Celebrate is a book about sharing good food and good times with the people we love. Food is at the heart of most celebrations, and for someone who follows a low-carb lifestyle, this can be a challenge. After living this way myself for many years, a celebrations book seemed like a natural progression. We've celebrated many occasions and holidays with all low-carb recipes. You can easily use either of my two other books to create wonderful menus for any occasion, but here my goal is to offer you even more recipes with a focus on celebratory fun.

This book is meant for every type of gathering, large or small, formal or casual. Most of the recipes serve six to eight people but can be scaled up to feed more. The chapters are organized in the way that I like to put meals together, by choosing from categories ranging from beverages to desserts. I've even included a chapter for brunch. This makes it simple to design a menu for your guests. This is for those of you who, like me, enjoy planning your own menus. Of course, I offer several preplanned menus for those who want that option, too.

Let's Celebrate includes over 115 carb-conscious recipes for every occasion. You'll find appetizers, soups, salads, main dishes, sides, desserts, and beverages, as well as practical notes and recommendations for doubling as needed. I encourage you not to be intimidated by cooking low-carb recipes for people who don't normally eat this way. I've done it for years and always get rave reviews! Everyone, no matter how they eat, appreciates good food and good company.

"Life is precious and should be celebrated."

Hospitality

Hospitality is defined as the generous reception and entertainment of guests, visitors, or strangers. In my first book, I speak a bit about my Southern heritage and Southern hospitality. We Southerners love to open our homes and serve up a good old-fashioned meal, and I grew up with an appreciation for our many gatherings of family and friends. My Grandma Ida would plan for weeks to feed our large family for a special occasion such as Christmas. I would watch her in the kitchen and admire how easy she made it seem—now I know it was not! She cooked amazing food, and I hoped I could be just like her someday.

When I got married, even though my husband and I lived in a tiny apartment, I couldn't wait to host our friends. We took pride in our small game-day get-togethers. Over the years, I threw many birthday parties, showers, and other gatherings—only back then, most of the recipes I made came from *Southern Living* magazines or church cookbooks that I proudly own to this day.

We're famous for our hospitality here in the South, but I've been lucky enough to experience the hospitality of people far and wide. Before the pandemic, I was invited to a book signing at the Luv ice cream shop in Saint Paul, Minnesota. I will never forget how Susanna, Ilya, and their team welcomed us with open arms. My friends and I were blown away by their kindness. It was a wonderful experience, and a reminder of the importance of connection.

Hospitality isn't about perfection. Celebrations don't have to be complicated or expensive. Whatever you do, just do it with heart. People will never forget how welcome you made them feel.

"*Hospitality is love in action.*"

Planning a Party

Planning is my favorite part of hosting any get-together. I love to find inspiration, think about menus, and make lists. If planning isn't your strong suit, ask for help! You can enlist the help of a friend or family member. Play to each other's strengths and don't let yourself get overwhelmed. It's always more fun to work together.

How soon you should begin planning depends on the size and formality of your event. You can find lots of ideas on websites like Pinterest, but make sure you're not overloaded with too much information at once. Come up with a plan, stick with it, and—most of all—have fun! In the end, it's about spending time with people you care about. However you choose to entertain, do it with joy. The rest will work itself out!

On the following page is a checklist you can use if you are hosting an event yourself. If you are planning a large celebration such as a wedding, you may want to hire professional help. Look for an event planner who can help you plan and organize your gathering. They will help you manage the planning, budget, and vision, obtain the supplies you need, and enlist people to carry out the necessary tasks.

"The best thing about memories...
is making them."

At least

1 MONTH AHEAD

- ☐ Choose a date and location.
- ☐ Plan your theme.
- ☐ Establish a budget.
- ☐ Prepare the guest list.
- ☐ Send invitations, whether handwritten or online.
- ☐ Buy any needed party décor.
- ☐ Rent, buy, or arrange to borrow any needed party equipment: tables, chairs, tents, etc.
- ☐ Start any DIY projects you have planned, such as centerpieces and place cards.
- ☐ Plan the menu. (If you intend to enlist the help of others, decide who will be bringing what.)
- ☐ Make a grocery list, then divide it into two lists: one for nonperishables and one for perishables.

1 WEEK AHEAD

- ☐ Shop for nonperishable groceries and paper goods.

2 DAYS AHEAD

- ☐ Clean the house and purchase all perishables.

1 DAY AHEAD

- ☐ Prepare the food that can be made ahead of time. (See notes in the individual recipes for specific make-ahead time frames.)
- ☐ Decorate and set the table(s) and/or buffet.

DAY OF THE GATHERING

- ☐ Prepare any food that needs to be made fresh.
- ☐ Buy and arrange fresh flowers, if using.
- ☐ Place the finishing touches on the décor.
- ☐ Take out the trash and empty the dishwasher to make for easier cleanup later.
- ☐ Reheat and display the food and prepare drinks.
- ☐ Welcome your guests and enjoy the party!

The atmosphere you create will impact the overall feel of your event. Music helps set the tone. You can pick your own playlist and pair it with Bluetooth speakers, or, if you want to go all out, you can hire a DJ. Nice lighting is relaxing, too. Turn off overhead lights and use candles and lower-wattage bulbs in lamps. When hosting an outdoor gathering at night, lanterns and strands of Edison-style lights add a nice touch. Tiki torches and stands are a favorite of mine. They also help repel insects!

Themed Menu Ideas

This book is filled with recipes that are perfect for gatherings and can be mixed and matched however you like. If you need some inspiration for crafting your celebratory menus, I've got you covered. Here I've put together some simple themed menus to make the process easier for you. Feel free to make substitutions. As I've said before, planning is the fun part!

Summer Picnic

128
Mini Salami
Cheese Balls

158
Antipasto Skewers

180
BLT Chicken Salad

— OR —

190
Shrimp Salad

246
Bacon Ranch
Fauxtato Salad

122
Crispy Crackers

— OR —

Store-bought
low-carb crackers

270
Dad's Strawberry
Fluff Salad

Iced tea

Mexican Fiesta

220 Cheesy Chicken & Rice

142 Large Batch Guacamole

132 Blender Salsa

138 Fiesta Layered Dip Cups

136 Restaurant-Style Queso Dip

66 Shaken Margarita

Low-carb tortillas or chips or pork rinds

Italian Soup & Salad Luncheon

126 Caesar Salad Parfaits

198 Creamy Tuscan Chicken Soup

242 Roasted Garlic & Herb Breadsticks

268 Tiramisu Mousse

Low-Carb Takeout

116 Crab Rangoon-Stuffed Mushrooms

194 Egg Roll Soup

212 Asian-Inspired Beef Cups

226 Sesame Chicken

Romantic Dinner

68

Frozen Peach
Bellini

124

Shrimp Cocktail
Cups

186

Blueberry & Feta
Arugula Salad

230

Bacon-Wrapped
Stuffed Pork
Tenderloin

254

Maple Bourbon
Brussels Sprouts

278

Double Chocolate
Bundt Cake

Holiday Dinner

152

Bacon Jalapeño
Deviled Eggs

140

Cheesy Hot
Crab Dip

224

Maple & Brown
Sugar-Glazed
Spiral Ham

256

Green Bean
Casserole with
Fried Onions

252

Loaded Roasted
Radishes

238

Hawaiian
Pull-Apart Rolls

284

Pecan Pumpkin
Crisp

82

Mulled Wine

Kid-Friendly Feast

72 Nonalcoholic Party Punch

150 Pepperoni Pizza Bites

170 Slow Cooker Party Meatballs

290 Vanilla Ice Cream

264 Cake Pops

Tailgate Party

130 Savory Party Snack Mix

114 Nashville Hot Peanuts

136 Restaurant-Style Queso Dip

162 Jalapeño Corn Dog Poppers

218 Parmesan Garlic Wings

196 Slow Cooker Chili for a Crowd

160 Everything Bagel Pigs in a Blanket

280 Better-Than-Anything Cake

Southern Comfort Spread

Iced tea

74
Blackberry
Mint Juleps

118
Baked Jalapeño
Pimento Cheese Dip

244
Creamy Cucumber
Salad

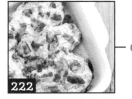
222
Loaded Ranch Pork
Chops

— OR —

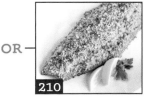
210
Pecan-Crusted
Salmon

252
Loaded Roasted
Radishes

248
Okra Fritters

270
Dad's Strawberry
Fluff Salad

Baby or Bridal Shower Brunch

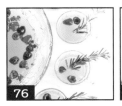
76
Champagne Punch

78
Mocha Punch

Bowl of mixed nuts

164
Personal
Charcuterie Boards

146
Praline Pecan Brie

154
Olive Pinwheels

166
Veggie Pizza

266
No-Bake
Cheesecake Cups

274
Chocolate Cream
Cheese Dip

Game Night

166
Veggie Pizza

162
Jalapeno Corn Dog Poppers

130
Savory Party Snack Mix

282
Turtle Pie

90
Arnold Palmer

Backyard Barbecue

152
Bacon Jalapeño Deviled Eggs

160
Everything Bagel Pigs in a Blanket

Hamburgers on low-carb buns

240
Cilantro Lime Coleslaw

— OR —

244
Creamy Cucumber Salad

286
Strawberry Shortcake Trifle

— OR —

264
Cake Pops

90
Arnold Palmer

Low-carb beers or mixed drinks

Chili Night

196
Slow Cooker Chili
for a Crowd

122
Crispy Crackers

— OR —

Store-bought
low-carb crackers

Low-carb
tortilla chips

142
Large Batch
Guacamole

Sliced green onions

Sliced jalapeños

Sour cream

Shredded cheddar
cheese

Book Club

140
Cheesy Hot
Crab Dip

146
Praline Pecan Brie

272
Creamy Vanilla
Yogurt Fruit Dip

Fresh berries

262
Lemon Ricotta
Cookies

82
Mulled Wine

What Can I Bring?

To potluck or not to potluck, that is the question. Some people are strongly against potlucks, but I'm quite fond of them. It takes the pressure off one person and really is the most practical, cost-efficient choice for feeding a crowd. It's customary for the host to provide the main dish(es) and beverages and for the guests to bring salads, sides, and desserts. I have wonderful childhood memories of large potluck dinners served at family gatherings and at church. There were always lots of hearty dishes and a dessert table loaded with cakes, cookies, and pies. Attending a potluck also ensures you can bring something to eat that fits your low-carb lifestyle.

If you are hosting a potluck, you can suggest specific dishes for your guests to bring and even provide the recipes. There are lots of ways for everyone to contribute, even if it's bringing the napkins, plates, and utensils.

Potluck Sign-Up Sheet

Please write your name next to a number and indicate what item you will be bringing to the potluck.

APPETIZERS

1. _____
2. _____
3. _____

SALADS

1. _____
2. _____
3. _____

BREAD/ROLLS/BUNS

1. _____
2. _____
3. _____

SIDE DISHES

1. _____
2. _____
3. _____

MAIN DISHES

1. _____
2. _____
3. _____
4. _____
5. _____

DESSERTS

1. _____
2. _____
3. _____

BEVERAGES

1. _____
2. _____
3. _____

OTHER GOODIES

1. _____
2. _____
3. _____

UTENSILS/DINNERWARE

1. Forks, spoons, & knives, _____ of each needed: _____

2. Serving spoons & spatulas, _____ of each needed: _____

3. Napkins, _____ of each needed: _____

4. Plates, _____ of each needed: _____

5. Cups, _____ of each needed: _____

Setting the Table

Dining etiquette dates back centuries, but nowadays setting a formal table is a bit of a lost art. It's a skill that simply hasn't been passed down to the younger generations, and as times have changed, families don't sit down to daily meals as often as they used to. When my husband and I got married, our first apartment had a tiny kitchen table with only two chairs. As our family and our space grew, so did my interest in decorating with dishes, linens, and such. My style isn't what I would consider formal, but I do love a nice place setting and a beautiful centerpiece.

When deciding how to set a table for a celebration, your choices should be based on your personality, what you enjoy, and the number of people you are entertaining. If you're hosting a small group of friends, for example, it's fun to plan a special place card or personalized memento at every seat.

Whether your style is casual or formal, the diagrams on the next two pages show you the proper way to arrange the plates, silverware, and glassware for a sit-down meal.

Casual

WATER GLASS

WINE GLASS

SALAD FORK

DINNER FORK

DINNER PLATE

NAPKIN

SALAD PLATE

DINNER KNIFE

TEASPOON

SOUP SPOON

Formal

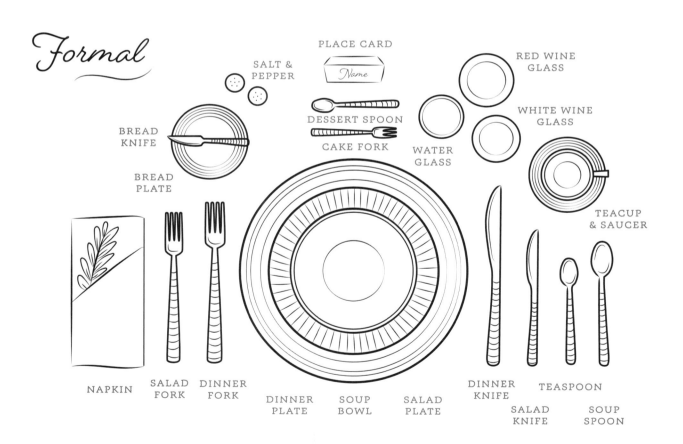

SALT & PEPPER

PLACE CARD

Name

RED WINE GLASS

DESSERT SPOON

CAKE FORK

WHITE WINE GLASS

BREAD KNIFE

WATER GLASS

BREAD PLATE

TEACUP & SAUCER

NAPKIN

SALAD FORK

DINNER FORK

DINNER PLATE

SOUP BOWL

SALAD PLATE

DINNER KNIFE

SALAD KNIFE

TEASPOON

SOUP SPOON

For a larger crowd, I prefer buffet-style, serve-yourself gatherings. Though inherently less formal, a buffet table can be arranged and decorated just as artfully as a dining table.

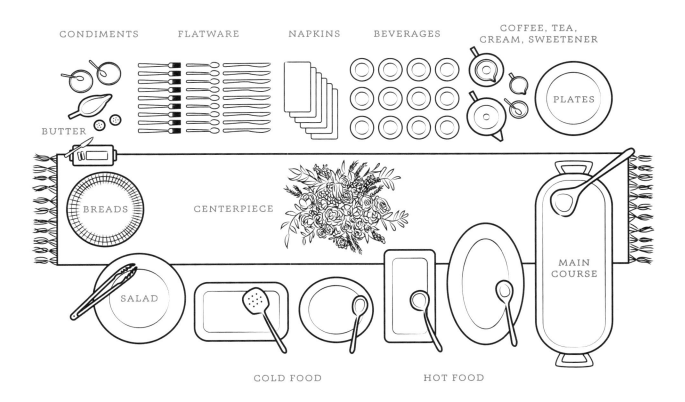

Serving Pieces and Décor

You may already own the essentials for entertaining, but not everyone has a china cabinet full of family heirlooms. I'd dare to say that these days, most modern homes don't even have a china cabinet! None of the items I recommend here are required, but they are nice to have for throwing a party. I suggest shopping for them at stores like Home Goods, IKEA, TJ Maxx, Pottery Barn, Williams Sonoma, and World Market. And let's not forget thrift stores! Being a good host doesn't have to cost a lot, and some of my best finds have come from thrift stores.

Don't feel like you have to buy everything at once—you can start small and collect things along the way. You can also borrow from friends and relatives. If you are hosting a larger gathering, consider renting from one of the many companies that specialize in these items, along with tents, tables, and chairs.

Wooden Serving Boards

Look for a range of shapes and sizes. Some of my favorite boards combine wood and marble for both function and aesthetics. While commonly used for charcuterie, I also use my boards for serving other finger foods, and I keep them propped up as kitchen décor when not in use.

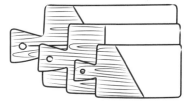

Serving Platters

White serving platters are easy to find. Look for oval and round platters in various sizes. It's also convenient to have a large platter with handles that's sturdy enough to carry a main dish.

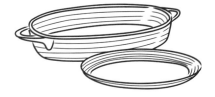

Serving Bowls

Serving bowls in many sizes are essential. White ceramic bowls are very versatile. Or, if you prefer, you can combine colors and patterns for an eclectic mix. Not everything has to match! A large wooden salad bowl with matching tongs will bring you enjoyment for years to come; it's super functional and really dresses up the table as well. A set of small bowls is great for serving condiments.

Chafing Dishes or Tray Warmers

Either chafing dishes or tray warmers will help you keep foods warm on the buffet table. These are needed items if you do much buffet-style entertaining! They use indirect heat to keep hot foods at serving temperature. Chafing dishes come in a variety of sizes and styles. Some are disposable metal, or, for a more elegant look, there's stainless steel.

Trifle Bowl

A trifle bowl might not seem like the most practical purchase, but it is a lot more adaptable than you think. A trifle bowl filled with a layered dessert makes a lovely centerpiece. You can also use it for layered salads and dips.

Cake Stand

In my opinion, you can never own too many cake stands. Cake stands of varying materials and sizes are nice to have and great for more than just cake. I enjoy using mine to display a variety of foods, both sweet and savory. When not in use, they make nice home décor, too.

Tablecloths and Napkins

Follow your tastes here and choose what you love. If you're more of a minimalist, you may prefer all-white tablecloths and napkins. Or you can mix and match different colors and patterns. Depending on your entertaining style and the formality of the event, you can go with real linens or purchase pretty paper napkins, paper tablecloths, and butcher paper from party stores.

White Dishware

You can't go wrong with classic white dishes. Almost every box store and home store sells an inexpensive set that can be dressed up or down depending on the occasion. You can also find attractive white plastic plates that resemble ceramic dishes at hobby and craft stores.

Glassware

Your choice of glassware depends on your needs. You'll want highball tumbler-style glasses for beverages such as water and iced tea, a set of stemware for wine, and mugs for coffee and cocoa. Highball and lowball glasses (aka rocks or old-fashioned glasses) are staples for cocktails, and you may wish to invest in specialty drinkware such as margarita glasses, champagne flutes, punch glasses, piña colada glasses, and/or julep cups. Besides drinks, I also use clear cups or glasses for pretty individual portions of appetizers, such as Shrimp Cocktail Cups (page 124) and Caesar Salad Parfaits (page 126). The best size for this purpose is 8 ounces.

Flatware and Serveware

If you inherited your grandmother's fine silverware, then use that. But if you don't want the hassle of caring for it or simply need more flatware, you can purchase an extra set at most big box and home stores or on Amazon.com. Many hobby stores carry heavy plastic flatware that looks very realistic and comes in silver and gold. You'll need serving spoons and forks along with several pairs of tongs. A classic cake knife and server can also be used for pies and will last for many years.

Cheese Knives

A small set of multipurpose cheese knives comes in handy for cheese and charcuterie boards, in addition to being aesthetically pleasing. I prefer the ones with metal or wooden handles.

Cocktail Toothpicks

Cocktail toothpicks are essential for serving appetizer foods that are too messy to be eaten with your hands, such as the Slow Cooker Party Meatballs on page 170. They're also nice to have for foods that are to be dipped and for charcuterie boards (see page 164). Longer toothpicks (4½ to 5 inches) are cute for Antipasto Skewers (see page 158).

Glass Carafe/Pitcher

A large glass carafe is a smart investment if you entertain a lot. If you have storage space for more than one, it's handy to have different shapes and sizes. Carafes are beautiful for serving sweet tea, lemonade, or sangria (see page 88). Smaller ones are nice for juices, mimosas (see page 70), or Bloody Marys (see page 80).

Beverage Dispenser with Spigot or Punch Bowl

A large beverage dispenser is a wonderful option for big-batch drinks such as my Nonalcoholic Party Punch on page 72. I also use it to serve water infused with lemons and limes. A 1.5-gallon capacity dispenser will serve most needs. For the Champagne Punch and Mocha Punch on pages 76 and 78, I use a 1.5-gallon punch bowl and a 1-gallon punch bowl, respectively.

Coffee Maker and Thermal Carafe

Having a thermal carafe is a great way to serve hot coffee to a crowd. It's a double-walled container usually made of stainless steel. A nice carafe can keep coffee hot for several hours. Fill your carafe(s) with coffee (you might want to offer both regular and decaf) and prepare your coffee maker with ground coffee and water so it's ready to go when you need to brew a fresh pot. Make sure to provide stirrers.

Cocktail Shaker with Built-In Strainer

Cocktail shakers are typically made of stainless steel. Using a shaker is the most efficient way to simultaneously chill and dilute a cocktail such as a margarita (see page 66). The strainer keeps the ice and other non-liquid ingredients out of the drink when pouring it into a glass.

Ice Bucket with Tongs or a Scoop

An ice bucket makes for a nice presentation if you plan to serve ice. Depending on the type of event you are hosting, you can also use an extra cooler for ice.

Candles and Candle Holders

I love classic white candles. No matter the occasion, they are an inexpensive way to add warmth and depth to the table. Choose pillar candles of various heights and thin candlesticks. Glass, wood, and metal are just a few of the options available for candle stands and holders.

Greenery, Flowers, and Vases

A variety of greenery and flowers makes a gorgeous statement. Fresh or artificial is fine. I prefer fresh flowers that can be picked up the day of a party, but most hobby and craft stores carry an array of artificial greenery such as eucalyptus, which goes well with all color schemes and looks nice on a table with an assortment of candles. Search Pinterest to find inspiration for centerpieces that fit your personal style.

Food Safety and Storage

There are a couple of fundamental rules of food safety to keep in mind when entertaining, particularly if the food is served buffet style: hot foods must be kept hot and cold foods kept cold. You can use slow cookers, chafing dishes, or warming trays to keep foods hot, and you can nestle dishes of cold foods in bowls or trays of ice.

It's best to prepare only as much food as you know you will need for the number of guests in attendance, but if you do end up with leftover perishables—and they've been safely kept hot or cold or have not sat out at room temperature for more than two hours (or one hour if it's very hot, such as at a backyard party in the summertime)—they can be stored in the refrigerator for up to four days or in the freezer for up to four months. If you will not be able to consume the leftovers within four days, freeze them immediately. Defrost them in the refrigerator and eat them within four days.

Serving Tip

To ensure that foods remain at the proper temperatures, hot or cold, prepare multiple smaller platters or dishes ahead of time, rather than one large portion, to be pulled out of the fridge or heated in the oven as needed to replenish the buffet.

Low-Carb Happy Hour

Grab your friends, favorite drinks, great food, and good music! The easiest way to serve cocktails at a party is to offer a signature drink. You can choose from the recipes in this book, beginning on page 64. You can then add wine and beer to round out the drink menu.

To make sure you have enough, a good rule of thumb is to allow for one or two drinks per person for the first hour and one drink per person for each hour after that. Be aware that drinks with hard alcohol should be consumed even more conservatively.

Alcohol Safety

One of your most important roles as host is to make sure your guests aren't overserved and unable to drive. When your guests arrive, make sure they understand that they must have designated drivers or rideshares available if they overindulge. Also encourage them to partake in the nonalcoholic selections you have provided (see pages 72, 78, 84, and 90).

Beer

Though a less-ideal choice than wine or liquor in terms of carbs, several beers are popular among people who follow a low-carb lifestyle. Here are just a few options, but be on the lookout for more as companies start to take notice of their customers who moderate their carb consumption.

- Budweiser Select
- Corona Premier
- Dogfish Head Slightly Mighty IPA
- Lagunitas Daytime IPA
- Michelob Ultra

Wine

Choose dry wines that are lower in sugar:

- Red wine (Cabernet Sauvignon, Merlot, Pinot Noir, Syrah)
- White wine (Chardonnay, Pinot Grigio, Sauvignon Blanc)
- Dry rosé wine (Cabernet Sauvignon, Grenache, Pinot Noir, Syrah, Tavel)
- Sparkling wine (brut Champagne, Prosecco)

Liquor and Mixers

Most liquors are zero-carb, but be wary of some exceptions. Stick with unflavored liquors that don't have any added sugar. When choosing a flavored liquor, make sure the label says "zero sugar." Diet colas, sparkling waters, low-sugar juices, and zero-sugar tonics all make for good low-carb mixers.

- Gin
- Rum
- Tequila
- Vodka
- Whiskey

Hard Seltzer

Hard seltzer has become very popular in the last few years. Some brands—but not all—are low-carb, so be sure to check the nutritional values listed on the label. Here are a couple that are known to be lower-carb, but even with these recommendations, you should still be careful. Ingredients can change, which can alter the carb count.

- Truly Hard Seltzer
- White Claw Hard Seltzer

Nonalcoholic Beverages

Make sure to offer some fun options for your guests who don't drink alcohol. Flavored sparkling water served in wine glasses and garnished with fresh fruit is a nice touch. There are several delicious options in the Drinks chapter, such as Arnold Palmer (page 90) and Nonalcoholic Party Punch (page 72). For coffee lovers, brew a fresh pot and offer heavy whipping cream or half-and-half, zero-sugar flavored creamers, low-carb sweeteners, and sugar-free flavored syrups.

Carb-Conscious Charcuterie

Charcuterie boards are very popular and deserve their own discussion here. They can easily be customized to fit the size of your gathering and most dietary needs, and, besides being delicious, they make an eye-catching centerpiece! Whether you decide to create Personal Charcuterie Boards (page 164) or make a large spread that your guests can share, the same general principles apply. Note that a carb-conscious board simply replaces grain crackers and sugary jams or high-carb fruits with low-carb alternatives.

Mini wooden boards are a really fun way to present charcuterie and its accompaniments. If you can't find boards like these for individual portions, try paper cones or cups or small Mason jars. Don't be afraid to get creative!

Here's how to put together a gorgeous and tasty charcuterie board:

- **Decide on serving style and gather serving utensils:** Depending on the size of your party, choose one or two large boards or several individual-sized boards. Alternatively, forgo the board and line the table or countertop with butcher paper. (If doing the latter, be sure to have small cutting boards available for anything that requires cutting to prevent damage to your table or counter.) Gather small bowls for items such as nuts, seeds, and olives. Cheese knives, small tongs, and cocktail toothpicks or forks are useful for serving.

- **Determine quantity and variety:** The stars of any charcuterie board are cured meats and cheeses. For an appetizer portion, allow for 1 to 2 ounces of meats per person, and the same quantity of cheeses per person (about 3 ounces total of meats and cheeses per person). Add other items—nuts, olives, etc.—to fill out the board(s) and make an appealing and bountiful presentation. Do your best to offer variety: for example, offer at least two types of cheese, ideally one soft and one firm, and at least a couple of types of cured meats, such as one spicy and one mild.

- Arrange the items on the board in this order:
  - Cheeses
  - Meats
  - Veggies
  - Berries
  - Nuts and seeds
  - Olives (green or black)
  - Low-carb jams, jellies, dips, or other spreads
  - Low-carb crackers or pork rinds
  - Garnishes such as fresh rosemary or parsley sprigs

Shopping List Examples

Soft & Firm Cheeses

- Blue cheese
- Brie
- Cheddar (aged)
- Feta
- Goat cheese
- Gruyère
- Provolone
- Smoked Gouda

Deli Meats

- Ham
- Pepperoni
- Prosciutto
- Roast beef
- Salami (Calabrese, Genoa, peppered)
- Turkey

Veggies

- Banana peppers
- Bell pepper slices
- Celery sticks
- Cucumber slices
- Mini dill pickles
- Mini sweet peppers
- Radish slices

Berries

- Blackberries
- Blueberries
- Raspberries
- Strawberries

Nuts & Seeds

- Almonds (California or Marcona)
- Macadamia nuts
- Pecans
- Pistachios
- Pumpkin seeds, shelled
- Sunflower seeds, shelled
- Walnuts

Miscellaneous

- Caramelized Onion Dip (page 120)
- Cheese crisps
- Crispy Crackers (page 122)
- Fresh herb sprigs, such as rosemary or parsley, for garnish
- Mini Salami Cheese Balls (page 128)
- Nashville Hot Peanuts (page 114)
- Pork rinds
- Sugar-free chocolate
- Sugar-free jams and jellies
- Whole-grain mustard

Shopping for Ingredients

Sweeteners

When I first started keto years ago, keto-friendly sweeteners were hard to find. Now, there are lots of options available in most grocery stores. Be aware that not all sugar-free sweeteners are created equal. It's important to look for those with a low glycemic index, meaning they will not raise your blood sugar. I try to stay away from artificial sweeteners, as I explain below.

Recommended Sweeteners

The following are the keto-friendly sweeteners that I use. Most of them come in granular and confectioners' (powdered) forms. If needed, you can use a clean coffee grinder or spice grinder to turn granular sweetener into powder. Nowadays, most sweeteners also come in a brown sugar substitute blend. With the exception of allulose, you can use whichever of these sweeteners you prefer when I call for simply "sweetener" in a recipe; just make sure to use the form specified (granular or confectioners').

- Allulose (granular)
- Erythritol and erythritol blends
- Monk fruit and monk fruit blends
- Stevia (granular)

Note ——————————————————

I always use allulose in ice cream because it keeps the ice cream soft and scoopable. Many people also use allulose as a 1:1 replacement for sugar, even though it isn't as sweet. You'll need 1⅓ cups of allulose to equal the sweetness of 1 cup of sugar, whereas erythritol, monk fruit, and stevia are equally as sweet as sugar.

Less Desirable Sweeteners

These artificial sweeteners are known to have unpleasant or dangerous side effects and can raise blood sugar levels in some people. Maltitol, for instance, has been found to cause headaches and stomach irritability.

- Aspartame
- Maltitol
- Saccharin
- Sucralose

High-Quality Oils and Fats

Not all oils are created equal. Some, such as vegetable, canola, corn, soy, and sunflower oil, are considered to be inflammatory (although not everyone agrees on this). The following is a list of the high-quality oils that I use the most.

- **Avocado oil:** This is the oil I use most frequently. It has a high smoke point, which makes it safe for frying. And it has a neutral flavor, which makes it very versatile.

- **Bacon drippings:** This fat is great for frying and adds a unique depth of flavor to what you are cooking.

- **Butter:** I use salted butter (Kerrygold is my favorite brand), but if you prefer, you can use unsalted and increase the amount of salt in each recipe slightly.

- **Coconut oil, refined:** This oil is suitable for frying because of its high smoke point. If you don't like the taste of coconut, the refined version is the way to go since most or all of the coconut flavor is removed in the refining process. For a coconutty-tasting oil with all of its health benefits intact, use unrefined (virgin) coconut oil. (It can be used for cooking as well, but only at moderate heat and in recipes where the coconut flavor will not be unwanted.)

- **Extra-virgin olive oil:** I enjoy using this flavorful oil for salad dressings and roasted veggies. I don't use it for frying because of its lower smoke point.

- **Ghee:** Because it's a kind of clarified butter, ghee can be a good alternative to butter for those who are sensitive to dairy and lactose. It also has a high smoke point, making it perfect for frying.

Grocery List

Use this list as a guide to organize your groceries and make shopping for ingredients easier.

PRODUCE
- ☐ _____
- ☐ _____
- ☐ _____
- ☐ _____
- ☐ _____
- ☐ _____
- ☐ _____
- ☐ _____
- ☐ _____

DAIRY/DELI
- ☐ _____
- ☐ _____
- ☐ _____
- ☐ _____
- ☐ _____
- ☐ _____

MEAT/EGGS
- ☐ _____
- ☐ _____
- ☐ _____
- ☐ _____
- ☐ _____
- ☐ _____

FROZEN FOODS
- ☐ _____
- ☐ _____
- ☐ _____
- ☐ _____
- ☐ _____
- ☐ _____
- ☐ _____

CANNED GOODS
- ☐ _____
- ☐ _____
- ☐ _____
- ☐ _____
- ☐ _____
- ☐ _____
- ☐ _____

BAKING
- ☐ _____
- ☐ _____
- ☐ _____
- ☐ _____
- ☐ _____
- ☐ _____

SPICES
- ☐ _____
- ☐ _____
- ☐ _____
- ☐ _____
- ☐ _____
- ☐ _____

BEVERAGES
- ☐ _____
- ☐ _____
- ☐ _____
- ☐ _____

OTHER GROCERIES
- ☐ _____
- ☐ _____
- ☐ _____
- ☐ _____

PAPER GOODS
- ☐ _____
- ☐ _____
- ☐ _____
- ☐ _____

Where I Shop

Where you shop will depend largely on where you live. Club stores like Costco and Sam's Club are fantastic places to buy foods for gatherings because they have large selections of bulk-priced meats, cheeses, vegetables, and wines. Here I've included food lists for those stores along with Aldi, Trader Joe's, Walmart, and Amazon.com.

Costco & Sam's Club

I'm grouping these two together because they are both club stores and carry similar items, including a wide variety of paper goods that you may need for a gathering. They rotate their stock frequently, so a product might be there today and gone tomorrow. Look for kitchen tools and serveware in the home section.

- 4505 Chicharrones
- Almond butter (natural)
- Almond flour (blanched)
- Avocado oil
- Avocados
- Bacon
- Berries
- Bone broth
- Canned chicken breast
- Champagne
- Chicken wings
- Coconut oil
- Coffee
- Cold brew coffee
- Crepini Egg Wraps
- Dips
- Egg bites
- Eggs
- English cucumbers

- Extra-virgin olive oil
- Folios Cheese Wraps
- Green nonstarchy vegetables
- Ground beef
- Guacamole
- Hamburger patties
- Hard-boiled eggs
- Heavy cream
- Hot dogs (uncured)
- Kerrygold butter
- Keto bread
- Keto ice cream
- Low-carb crackers
- Low-carb tortillas
- Lump crab meat
- Lunch meats (uncured, nitrate-free)
- Marinara sauce (low-sugar)
- Mayonnaise

- Meat and cheese trays (premade)
- Moon Cheese
- Natural almond butter
- Nuts and seeds
- Parmesan crisps
- Pork belly
- Pork chops
- Pork ribs
- Pork rind crumbs
- Pork rinds (large containers)
- Pork tenderloin
- Produce (buy in bulk)
- Pure vanilla extract
- Riced cauliflower (fresh and frozen)
- Rotisserie chicken
- Salami
- Salsa (organic)
- Sausages
- Specialty cheeses (hard and sliced)
- Spices (buy in bulk)
- Spiral ham
- Steaks
- Sugar-free BBQ sauce
- Sweeteners
- Sugar-free chocolate chips
- Wild Alaskan salmon
- Wine

Aldi

Aldi is one of my favorite budget-friendly grocery stores. Shop there for quality meats and cheeses for your charcuterie boards. Be sure to check the seasonal aisle for serving pieces, too. I've even found nice bar sets and ice buckets at Aldi.

- Apple cider vinegar (organic)
- Avocado oil
- Bacon
- Biltong beef jerky
- Butter
- Champagne
- Cream cheese
- Crepini Egg Wraps
- Dilly Bites dill pickles
- Egg Life Egg Wraps
- Eggs
- Everything bagel seasoning
- Extra-virgin olive oil
- Folios Cheese Wraps
- Ghee
- Heavy cream
- Keto bread
- Keto ice cream
- Low-carb crackers
- Low-carb tortillas
- Lunch meats (uncured, nitrate-free)
- Meats
- Nuts and seeds
- Parmesan crisps
- Peanut butter (organic)
- Pepperoni
- Pork rinds
- Produce (organic)
- Prosciutto
- Riced cauliflower (frozen)
- Salami
- Sausage
- Sour cream
- Specialty cheeses (hard and sliced)
- Sweeteners
- Two Good Greek yogurt
- Wine

Trader Joe's

Trader Joe's is another affordable grocery store that's known for its high-quality products. If you're on social media, you'll notice the brand has attracted a cultlike following. They sell lots of unique products and seasoning blends that keep you wondering what they'll come up with next!

- Almond flour (blanched)
- Avocado oil
- Avocados
- Bacon (slices and ends and pieces)
- Baking powder (aluminum-free)
- Beef sticks
- Bell peppers
- Berries
- Bone broth
- Broth (organic)
- Brussels sprouts
- Cauliflower thins
- Champagne
- Cheese bites
- Coconut aminos
- Coconut flour
- Coconut oil
- Dips and spreads
- Eggs
- Extra-virgin olive oil
- Ghee
- Green nonstarchy vegetables
- Hard-boiled eggs
- Hearts of palm pasta
- Heavy cream
- Kerrygold butter
- Mascarpone cheese
- Meats for charcuterie
- Mini sweet peppers
- Natural peanut butter (organic)
- Nuts
- Olives
- Riced cauliflower (fresh or frozen)
- Seasoning blends: 21 Seasoning Salute, dill pickle seasoning, everyday seasoning, Everything but the Bagel seasoning, garlic salt, ranch seasoning, seasoning salt, umami seasoning
- Sparkling water
- Specialty cheeses (soft, hard, and sliced)
- Sweeteners
- Taco sauce
- Toasted sesame oil
- Unsweetened cocoa powder
- Unsweetened coconut flakes
- Wine

Walmart

Walmart has really stepped it up in the low-carb department over the past few years. I can find almost everything I need here, and their prices are usually good. It's also a store that's accessible to many people who live in smaller communities.

- Almond milk
- Avocado oil
- Bacon
- Broth (organic)
- Butter (organic)
- Champagne
- Cheese crisps
- Coconut flour
- Coconut milk
- Coconut oil
- Cream cheese
- Eggs
- Ghee
- Hearts of palm pasta
- Heavy cream

- Isopure unflavored whey protein isolate
- Keto bread
- Keto ice cream
- Keto yogurt
- Low-carb crackers
- Low-carb tortillas
- Marinara sauce (low-sugar)
- Nuts and seeds
- Pork rinds
- Rotisserie chicken
- Sugar-free chocolate chips
- Sweeteners (including allulose)
- Wine
- Xanthan gum

Note

I do not use Walmart's Great Value almond flour. I have tried it a few times with less than desirable results.

Amazon.com

Items that you can't find at your local grocery store can usually be ordered from Amazon.com. It's also a good place to shop for kitchen items, entertaining essentials, and party supplies.

- Almond flour (blanched)
- Coconut flour
- Flavored extracts (such as corn and pineapple)
- Good Dee's sugar-free sprinkles
- Hilo tortilla chips
- Isopure unflavored whey protein isolate
- Pork panko (pork rind crumbs)
- Quest tortilla chips
- Sugar-free chocolate chips
- Sweeteners (including allulose)
- Xanthan gum

Nonfood items:

- Cake pop sticks
- Cocktail toothpicks
- Wooden or bamboo skewers

How Much to Buy?

When planning quantities of food for a party, I suggest you try to estimate as closely as possible (while erring on the side of too much rather than too little!) the amount that will be consumed by your guests to minimize leftovers. The recipes in this book typically serve six to eight people and assume that everyone will help themselves to a small portion from each dish. Serving several dishes at a time will feed more people.

My Favorite Kitchen Equipment

I love kitchen gadgets and small appliances of all kinds. I sometimes have to stop myself from buying more! Here, I've narrowed it down to a list of my most-used items for cooking and baking. This list assumes your kitchen is already equipped with basics such as a set of pots and pans, mixing bowls, mixing spoons, and spatulas.

Baking Dishes

Ceramic baking dishes that can go from oven to table are
essential for casseroles. My most used sizes are 9-inch square,
11 by 7-inch, and 13 by 9-inch.

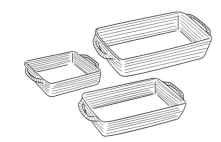

Baking Sheets (aka Cookie Sheets)

I use standard 18 by 12-inch flat baking sheets for biscuits
and cookies.

Blender

I frequently use my Blendtec blender for smoothies and cocktails. It's a pricier
brand but has been worth it to me because of its high-powered blending
capabilities. It can even be used to make nut butters and sauces. That said, a
standard blender will do the trick for all of the recipes in this book. (You just
may have to blend longer!) For these recipes, you will need a standard-size
blender or larger.

Bundt Pan

I own several Bundt pans and would surely have more if storage space
wasn't an issue! There are so many patterns to choose from. These pans
are great for cakes, obviously, but can also be used for meatloaf and
pull-apart breads and as a mold to make an ice ring for punch. For the
recipes in this book, you'll need a 12-cup Bundt pan.

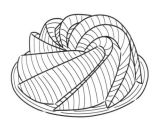

Cast-Iron Skillet

Every kitchen needs at least one cast-iron skillet. For the recipes in this
book, you'll need a 10-inch skillet, but a 12-inch skillet is a great size
to own as well. Cast iron is durable, holds heat well, and improves with
age by becoming more seasoned. I like how easily it goes from stovetop
to oven. When well cared for, a cast-iron skillet can last for generations.

Food Processor

Though not a must-have, a food processor is a handy appliance if you cook a lot. It makes prep work like chopping, shredding, and slicing easier. You can also use it to make purees and sauces. I recommend an 8-cup food processor, but the 4-cup size works just as well for most smaller jobs.

Large Deep Skillet

A large deep skillet is great for one-pan meals. I use a Calphalon 13-inch skillet with 4¾-inch sides.

Meat Thermometer

This tool is important for measuring the internal temperature of meat. Thermometers come in a variety of models; some of the fancier ones have an electronic sensor and apps they can be paired with.

Mesh Skimmer

This inexpensive tool makes it easier and safer to remove foods from hot oil when frying. It can also be used to drain canned foods.

Muffin Pans (Standard and Mini)

A standard-size 12-well muffin pan is essential, and not just for muffins. I use mine to create single-serving quiches, meatloaves, and pies. A 24-well mini muffin pan is fun to have as well and is perfect for making bite-size morsels of food to accompany the cocktail hour, like Pepperoni Pizza Bites (page 150) or Quiche Lorraine bites (page 94).

Parchment Paper

I use parchment paper almost daily in my kitchen. It prevents sticking and makes cleanup a breeze. Be careful not to confuse it with wax paper, which is not oven-safe like parchment is. If you don't have parchment paper on hand, you can almost always use aluminum foil or grease the pan instead. Silicone baking mats are also a good alternative.

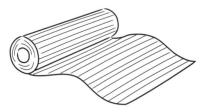

Pie Plate

Pie plates can be used for sweet and savory pies such as quiches. The standard size is 9 inches. These can be made of glass, ceramic, or aluminum, but I tend to use my ceramic pie plate the most.

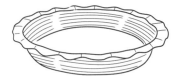

Quality Knives

There's nothing like a sharp, quality knife to make prep work a breeze. If you've ever used a dull knife, then you know! A dull knife can also be dangerous, so invest in the best knives you can afford, keep them sharpened, and never put them in the dishwasher. Moderately priced knives will last if you care for them properly.

Roasting Pan with Rack

I use a roasting pan for larger cuts of meat, such as the glazed ham on page 224. The rack allows the meat to sit above the fat and drippings while the tall sides help prevent these liquids from spilling in the oven.

Sheet Pans (aka Rimmed Baking Sheets)

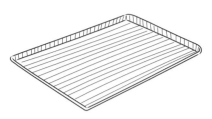

These pans are a real necessity in my kitchen; I use them almost every day for sheet pan dinners, roasted vegetables, pizza, and so much more. I own a number of sheet pans, some purchased at thrift stores. I love the look of a well-aged sheet pan. I have a few different sizes, but the standard is 18 by 13 inches.

Silicone Baking Cups

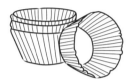

Silicone is nice because nothing sticks to it. It's also reusable, which makes silicone baking cups more cost-effective than paper liners over time. Try using them as dividers in lunch boxes, too.

Slow Cooker

The slow cooker has long been a favorite of busy families. This inexpensive appliance is well suited for cheaper cuts of meat because low and slow cooking tenderizes meat and brings out the flavor. I recommend the 6-quart size. A slow cooker can also be used for serving, keeping foods warm and at a safe temperature.

Stand Mixer or Hand Mixer

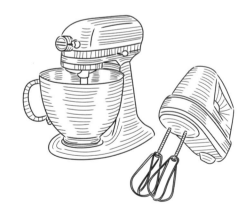

My KitchenAid stand mixer is without a doubt my favorite kitchen appliance. I've owned it for almost two decades, so at this point it's practically part of the family. It was an investment but has paid off over time. It makes big mixing jobs so much easier. If you don't have a stand mixer, you can make all of the recipes in this book using an electric hand mixer, which is less expensive and easier to clean and store. For accessibility, I specify a hand mixer in the recipes; however, either type of mixer is fine to use.

Stockpot or Dutch Oven

A 6-quart stockpot or Dutch oven is the most versatile size, perfect for soups, stews, and deep-frying. A stainless-steel stockpot or uncoated cast-iron Dutch oven is just fine, but I like enameled cast-iron Dutch ovens because they are easier to clean than uncoated cast iron, and they're attractive enough to set out on a buffet, placed on some sort of warming device. Lodge offers a lower-priced option, while Staub and Le Creuset are popular higher-end brands.

Whipped Cream Dispenser

Why buy a whipped cream dispenser when you can buy a can of whipped cream at the grocery store, you ask? Hands down, fresh whipped cream with no preservatives or chemicals just tastes better—and lets you control the amount and type of sweetener and flavorings added. I like liquid stevia and vanilla extract, but you can experiment with a variety of flavored extracts. The decorative tips make for a nice presentation. Look for a dispenser with metal tips and threads, which tend to last longer than plastic ones. Of course, you could make homemade whipped cream the old-fashioned way, with a bowl and a hand mixer (see page 296), but this handy dispenser does it for you in a fraction of the time.

RECIPES

About the Recipes

The following chapters contain over 115 low-carb adaptations of some of my favorite dishes that you can use to create menus for your most special occasions. My family and friends have enjoyed every one of these recipes, and they've become staples at our gatherings. I hope you like them as much as we do!

I've marked the recipes with handy icons:

Contains dairy

Contains eggs

Contains nuts

Contains peanuts

Quick & easy—can be made in under 30 minutes (although some require extra time for chilling, etc., before they are ready to serve)

For a handy chart showing which recipes fall into these categories, see pages 314 to 316.

Make Ahead Tips

To help you make efficient use of your time, I've noted when an entire recipe or a part of a recipe can be made in advance. Look for the practical tips below the recipe explaining how many days in advance the recipe (or part of it) can be made and how it should be stored and reheated, if needed.

Nutrition Info

I've included nutrition information for every recipe as well. I calculated it to the best of my ability, using my preferred brands of ingredients. Optional ingredients are not included in these numbers. Oil used for frying is also omitted because there is no way to accurately calculate the amount absorbed. I always recommend calculating your own macros, as they can vary widely depending on the brands of ingredients you select. There are many apps you can use for this task.

Doubling Recipes

If you're throwing a larger party, you may need to double one or more of the recipes on your menu. Most of the recipes in this book serve six to eight people, but of course each one will go further if you're serving several dishes for a buffet spread. It's not always as simple as doubling the ingredients. This approach does work well with soups and casseroles, but it can be trickier when it comes to baked goods; in some cases it's better to make multiple batches.

When doubling a recipe, please keep the following tips in mind:

- Determine the sizes and number of pots and pans and mixing bowls (and so on) you will need. For example, if meat is to be browned in a medium-size skillet, use a large or even extra-large skillet; if the ingredients for a marinade are mixed in a medium-size mixing bowl, use a large one instead. If a recipe requires one sheet pan or muffin pan, plan to use two.

- For best results, use two baking dishes or pans of the same size specified in the recipe rather than one larger dish or pan to contain the doubled quantity of food. Baking the doubled quantity in one larger baking dish would greatly affect the cooking time and the success of the recipe. Because the recipes have not been tested using pan or dish sizes other than those specified, I do not recommend you use a larger size.

- When baking more than one dish or pan of food, it's best to place them side by side, but not touching, on the middle rack in the oven. To ensure even baking, rotate the dishes midway through baking. If baking a cake, wait to open the oven door until about two-thirds through baking. If the pans/ dishes won't fit side by side on the same rack, place one on the middle rack and the second on the rack just below it. They should be off-center, not stacked one atop the other. Once or twice during baking, switch the pans and rotate them as well.

- When doubling recipes, the cook time may increase slightly. This is particularly true for baked foods since some heat will be lost when you open the oven door to switch or rotate pans. For this reason, pay close attention to the description provided to help you determine doneness rather than relying on the stated cook times.

- Cook or fry food in as many batches as needed to avoid crowding the pan and to ensure it browns or crisps properly. For example, if a recipe calls for browning meat in a large skillet, you will need to brown the doubled quantity in two batches. If a recipe calls for spreading food on a sheet pan, don't try to fit the doubled quantity in one pan; instead, use two pans.

CHAPTER 1
Drinks

Shaken Margarita

yield one 8-ounce serving • *prep time* 5 minutes

Ice

3 ounces silver tequila

2 ounces freshly squeezed lime juice

1 teaspoon pure orange extract

5 drops liquid stevia

2 ounces orange sparkling water

1 lime wedge, for garnish

For the rim:

Kosher salt

Lime slice

1. Fill a cocktail shaker with ice. Add the tequila, lime juice, orange extract, and stevia. Cover and shake vigorously to mix, about 30 seconds.

2. To rim the glass, sprinkle some kosher salt on a small plate. Use the lime slice to moisten the rim of a 9-ounce glass (preferably a margarita glass) and press the rim into the salt to coat.

3. Fill the glass with ice. Strain the margarita into the glass, top it off with the sparkling water, and garnish with the lime wedge.

Note

The addition of sparkling water makes this margarita lighter than classic versions; if you'd like a more traditional drink, omit it.

NET CARBS 5.2g

calories	fat	protein	carbs	fiber
246	0.1g	0.3g	5.6g	0.5g

Frozen Peach Bellini

yield four 8-ounce servings • *prep time* 10 minutes

1 medium peach, peeled, pitted, and sliced

1 tablespoon freshly squeezed lemon juice

1 tablespoon confectioners' sweetener

1 (750-ml) bottle Prosecco

2 cups ice

For garnish:

Fresh raspberries

Fresh mint leaves

Special equipment: Cocktail picks

Place the peach slices, lemon juice, sweetener, Prosecco, and ice in a blender. Blend on high speed until smooth. Pour into four 8-ounce glasses and serve immediately, garnished with raspberries and mint.

Note

Peaches aren't typical on a low-carb menu, but some people enjoy this sweet fruit in moderation, as in this refreshing fizzy drink.

NET CARBS 3.9g

calories	fat	protein	carbs	fiber
39	0.1g	0.4g	4.5g	0.6g

Reduced-Sugar Mimosa

yield six 6-ounce servings • *prep time* 5 minutes

1 (750-ml) bottle brut Champagne or other dry sparkling wine

½ cup low-sugar orange juice

For garnish:

Fresh berries of choice

Fresh mint leaves

Have on hand six 6-ounce champagne flutes. To build the drinks, take a flute and, while holding it at a slight tilt, pour in the Champagne until the glass is three-quarters full. Pour 1 tablespoon of the orange juice into the flute and garnish with berries and a mint leaf. Repeat with the remaining flutes to make a total of 6 mimosas.

Note

You can find low-sugar orange juice alongside the regular orange juice in the grocery store. I use Simply Light Orange Pulp Free.

NET CARBS 4.1g				
calories	fat	protein	carbs	fiber
103	0g	0.2g	4.1g	0g

Nonalcoholic Party Punch

yield twelve 8-ounce servings • *prep time* 10 minutes

Juice of 2 limes

¼ cup confectioners' sweetener

1 (2-liter) bottle diet ginger ale

3 cups diet cranberry juice drink

1 cup low-sugar orange juice (see Note, page 70)

2 teaspoons pure pineapple extract

Lime slices, for the beverage dispenser and for garnish

Ice, for serving

1. In a 1.5-gallon beverage dispenser or serving pitcher, stir together the lime juice and sweetener until the sweetener is dissolved.

2. Pour in the ginger ale, cranberry juice drink, orange juice, and pineapple extract. Stir until the ingredients are well combined. Add some lime slices to the dispenser or pitcher. Serve the punch in ice-filled 8-ounce glasses, garnished with additional lime slices.

Note

You can find diet cranberry juice drink next to the regular cranberry juice in the grocery store. I use Ocean Spray Diet Cranberry Juice Drink. You can find pure pineapple extract on Amazon.com.

NET CARBS 1.6g

calories	fat	protein	carbs	fiber
7	0g	0.1g	1.7g	0g

Blackberry Mint Julep

yield one 12-ounce serving • *prep time* 5 minutes

6 to 8 fresh mint leaves, torn, plus more for garnish if desired

6 blackberries, plus more for garnish if desired

1 tablespoon confectioners' sweetener

Crushed ice

2 ounces bourbon

1. In a 12-ounce julep cup or rocks glass, muddle the mint, blackberries, and sweetener until the sweetener is dissolved.

2. Mound the cup with crushed ice. Pour the bourbon over the ice and use a bar spoon to mix the bourbon and ice. Serve garnished with more blackberries and mint leaves, if desired.

Note

A muddler is a bar tool designed to crush aromatics and fresh fruit, such as herbs or berries, in a glass. It's shaped like a wand, rounded on one end to make it easy to hold and flat on the other end for greater crushing area. If you don't have one, you can use a wooden spoon. A bar spoon is a long spoon that allows you to reach the bottom of a tall drink, while its twisted handle facilitates stirring. If you don't have one, use an iced tea spoon.

Make Ahead

Mint juleps are always made painstakingly one by one. But if you're planning to serve more than one or two at a time, you can streamline the process by completing Step 1 before your guests arrive, using several julep cups. Then, when your guests arrive, all you need to do is add the ice, bourbon, and garnish.

NET CARBS 1.9g

calories	fat	protein	carbs	fiber
147	0.2g	0.6g	4.2g	2.3g

Champagne Punch

yield fourteen 8-ounce servings • *prep time* 10 minutes

1 (750-ml) bottle brut Champagne or other dry sparkling wine, chilled overnight

1 (2-liter) bottle diet ginger ale, chilled overnight

4 ounces vodka, chilled overnight

1 tablespoon pure orange extract

1 cup frozen raspberries

For garnish:

Fresh raspberries

Fresh rosemary sprigs

Pour the chilled Champagne into a 1.5-gallon punch bowl. Slowly pour in the chilled ginger ale. Stir in the chilled vodka and the orange extract until the punch is well blended. Add the frozen raspberries to the punch. Serve in punch glasses, garnished with fresh raspberries and rosemary sprigs.

Note

Don't forget to pop your bottles of sparkling wine, ginger ale, and vodka in the refrigerator the night before you plan to make the punch to ensure they are thoroughly chilled.

NET CARBS 1.8g

calories	fat	protein	carbs	fiber
64	0g	0.2g	2.1g	0.3g

Mocha Punch

yield eight 8-ounce servings • *prep time* 10 minutes, plus overnight to chill espresso mixture

4 cups water

½ cup instant espresso powder

¼ cup cocoa powder

¾ cup granular sweetener

1 cup unsweetened almond milk, chilled

1 cup heavy whipping cream

1 (16-ounce) container keto chocolate ice cream

Whipped Cream (page 296), for garnish (optional)

1. In a medium-size saucepan, bring the water to a boil. Remove the pan from the heat and stir in the espresso powder, cocoa powder, and sweetener until dissolved. Allow to cool completely, then cover and refrigerate overnight.

2. Pour the espresso mixture into a gallon-size punch bowl. Stir in the almond milk and cream until well combined. Use a scoop to drop scoops of the ice cream evenly across the punch. Allow to sit for 10 to 15 minutes before serving so the ice cream becomes melty.

3. Ladle the punch into 8-ounce punch glasses or glass coffee mugs. Garnish with whipped cream, if desired.

Note

This recipe is very special to me. For many years, long before going keto, I would make this punch for special occasions. It was always a favorite among friends, and once someone even asked me to make it for a wedding. I'm so happy to have created a low-carb version for this book that is just as delicious as the original!

NET CARBS 2.1g

calories	fat	protein	carbs	fiber
118	13.2g	1.1g	3.5g	1.5g

Bloody Mary Bar

yield eight 8-ounce servings • *prep time* 15 minutes

Bloody Mary mix:

1 (46-ounce) bottle tomato-vegetable juice, chilled

½ cup dill pickle juice

3 tablespoons Worcestershire sauce

3 tablespoons prepared horseradish

1 teaspoon Tabasco sauce

2 teaspoons celery salt

1 teaspoon ground black pepper

½ teaspoon smoked paprika

Rim salt:

2 tablespoons kosher salt

2 teaspoons smoked paprika

1 teaspoon celery salt

Lemon or lime wedges, for rimming the glasses

Ice, for serving

1 pint vodka

Suggested garnishes:

Cooked bacon slices, celery sticks, salami slices, olives, banana peppers, and/or cheese cubes

Special equipment: Cocktail picks

1. To make the Bloody Mary mix, pour the vegetable juice into a 40-ounce serving pitcher. Add the rest of the mix ingredients and stir until thoroughly combined. Refrigerate until ready to serve.

2. To make the rim salt, stir together the kosher salt, smoked paprika, and celery salt in a small mixing bowl. Store covered until ready to serve.

3. To build a drink, pour the rim salt onto a small plate. Rub the edge of a lemon or lime wedge around the rim of a tall 10-ounce glass to moisten it, then dip the rim into the rim salt, rolling it from side to side, making sure the rim is coated. Carefully fill the rimmed glass two-thirds full with ice, doing your best to avoid knocking the rim salt off.

4. Give the Bloody Mary mix a quick stir, then pour 6 ounces of the mix into the iced glass. Pour in 2 ounces of vodka and stir to combine. Invite your guests to add the garnishes of their choice to their drinks.

Make Ahead

For the best flavor, make the Bloody Mary mix no more than 2 days ahead. The glasses can be rimmed an hour or two before guests arrive. Any leftover mix can be stored in the refrigerator, covered with a lid, for up to a week. Discard any leftover rim salt.

	NET CARBS 5.8g			
calories	fat	protein	carbs	fiber
164	0.1g	1.4g	7.4g	1.6g

Mulled Wine

yield five 6-ounce servings • *prep time* 10 minutes • *cook time* 30 minutes

1 (750-ml) bottle dry red wine

3 or 4 large strips orange zest, plus more for garnish if desired

3 cinnamon sticks, plus more for garnish if desired

2 star anise pods, plus more for garnish if desired

2 tablespoons granular sweetener

1 teaspoon apple pie spice

¼ teaspoon ground nutmeg

1 teaspoon pure orange extract

¼ cup brandy (optional)

Fresh rosemary sprigs, for garnish

1. In a large nonreactive pot, combine the wine, orange zest, cinnamon sticks, anise pods, sweetener, apple pie spice, and nutmeg. Bring to a simmer over medium heat, then reduce the heat to low and simmer gently for 30 minutes, ensuring that it doesn't boil. Stir in the orange extract and the brandy, if using.

2. Remove from the heat and use a fine-mesh sieve to strain the solids from the wine. Serve in 6-ounce mugs. Garnish with orange zest strips, rosemary sprigs, cinnamon sticks, and/or anise pods, if desired.

Note

When zesting the orange, remove only the colored portion of the skin and avoid the pith (the white part), which would cause the mulled wine to be bitter. For buffet-style serving, pour the mulled wine into a slow cooker and set the temperature to warm.

Make Ahead

Can be made up to 2 days ahead. After straining the mulled wine in Step 2, allow to cool, then refrigerate until ready to use. Before serving, very gently warm the wine over the lowest heat possible or in a slow cooker set to low.

NET CARBS 3.6g

calories	fat	protein	carbs	fiber
223	0g	0.1g	3.6g	0g

Hot Cocoa for a Crowd

yield eight 6-ounce servings • *prep time* 10 minutes • *cook time* 2 hours

4 cups unsweetened almond milk

2 cups heavy whipping cream

½ cup cocoa powder

½ cup granular sweetener

1 cup sugar-free milk chocolate chips, plus more for garnish if desired

1 teaspoon pure vanilla extract

Whipped Cream (page 296), for garnish (optional)

1. Combine the almond milk and cream in a medium-size microwave-safe mixing bowl. Microwave on high in 1-minute increments until hot but not boiling.

2. Pour the milk mixture into a 6-quart slow cooker. Vigorously whisk in the cocoa powder and sweetener until mostly dissolved. Stir in the chocolate chips and vanilla.

3. Place the lid on the slow cooker and cook on low for 2 hours, stirring occasionally to ensure the chocolate chips are incorporated. Turn the temperature to warm.

4. Serve in mugs, garnished with whipped cream and chocolate chips, if desired.

NET CARBS 4.8g

calories	fat	protein	carbs	fiber
286	28.8g	3.3g	13.6g	8.8g

Piña Colada

yield two 8-ounce servings • *prep time* 10 minutes

½ cup full-fat canned coconut milk

¼ cup heavy whipping cream

2 tablespoons unsweetened shredded coconut

3 ounces light rum

2 tablespoons confectioners' sweetener

2 teaspoons pure pineapple extract

1½ cups ice

Place all of the ingredients in a blender and blend on high speed until smooth. Serve immediately in 8-ounce glasses.

Note

Can be doubled using a standard-size blender.

	NET CARBS 2.7g			
calories	fat	protein	carbs	fiber
327	23.5g	2.4g	3.7g	1g

Bubbly Sangria

yield ten 8-ounce servings • *prep time* 10 minutes, plus 6 hours to chill

1 lemon, sliced

1 lime, sliced

¼ cup blueberries

¼ cup raspberries

¼ cup sliced strawberries

1 (750-ml) bottle dry white wine

1 (750-ml) bottle Prosecco

12 ounces orange-flavored sparkling water

Ice, for serving

1. Place all of the fruit in a 4-quart serving pitcher. Add the wine and stir. Cover and refrigerate for at least 6 hours.

2. Before serving, add the Prosecco and sparkling water. Stir and serve over ice.

Note

If you prefer a sweeter sangria, you can add liquid sweetener to taste.

Make Ahead

Complete Step 1 up to 1 day ahead. Stir in the Prosecco and sparkling water right before serving.

NET CARBS 4.8g

calories	fat	protein	carbs	fiber
124	0.1g	0.3g	5.3g	0.5g

Arnold Palmer

yield eight 8-ounce servings • *prep time* 10 minutes, plus time to steep tea

Tea:
4 cups water
5 bags black tea

Lemonade:
4 cups water
¾ cup granular sweetener
Juice of 6 lemons

12 lemon slices, for the pitcher and for garnish

1. To make the tea, bring the water to a boil in a medium-size saucepan over medium heat. Turn off the heat. Add the teabags to the water and remove the pan from the burner. Let steep for 15 minutes. Squeeze the tea bags and remove them. Allow the tea to cool.

2. To make the lemonade, bring the water to a boil in a medium-size saucepan over medium heat. Add the sweetener and stir until completely dissolved. Remove the pan from the heat and stir in the lemon juice. Allow the lemonade to cool.

3. Pour the tea and lemonade into a 4-quart serving pitcher and stir to combine. Add 4 lemon slices to the pitcher. Serve over ice and garnish with the remaining lemon slices.

Make Ahead
Can be made up to 1 day ahead.

NET CARBS 1.8g

calories	fat	protein	carbs	fiber
6	0.1g	0.1g	1.9g	0.1g

Brunch

Quiche Lorraine—Two Ways

yield 1 large quiche or 24 bites (8 servings, 3 bites per serving) • *prep time* 10 minutes • *cook time* 30 minutes

2 tablespoons salted butter

¼ cup chopped onions

4 slices bacon, chopped

4 large eggs

1 cup heavy whipping cream

½ teaspoon salt

½ teaspoon ground black pepper

¼ teaspoon ground nutmeg

½ cup shredded Gruyère cheese

Chopped fresh parsley, for garnish

1. Preheat the oven to 350°F. If making one large quiche, lightly spray a 9-inch pie plate with oil; if making quiche bites, lightly spray the wells of a 24-well mini muffin pan.

2. Melt the butter in a medium-size skillet over medium heat. Add the onions and bacon and cook until the onions are soft and the bacon is crispy. Use a slotted spoon to remove the onions and bacon from the pan and set aside.

3. Whisk the eggs in a medium-size mixing bowl, then add the cream, salt, pepper, and nutmeg. Stir until well combined. Stir in the cooked bacon mixture and the cheese.

4. Pour the filling into the prepared pie plate or muffin pan, filling each muffin well about three-quarters full.

5. Bake until the center of the quiche is set and the top is lightly browned, 30 to 35 minutes for a large quiche or 15 to 20 minutes for quiche bites. Garnish with parsley and serve. Best eaten the same day.

Note

There are many ways to serve this quiche. The bites are great for brunch, but they also make a nice appetizer or addition to a grazing table.

	NET CARBS 0.7g			
calories	fat	protein	carbs	fiber
221	21g	8.4g	0.9g	0.3g

Bacon Cheddar Muffins

yield 10 muffins (1 per serving) • *prep time* 10 minutes • *cook time* 25 minutes

2 cups finely ground blanched almond flour

2 tablespoons granular sweetener

2 teaspoons baking powder

½ teaspoon salt

½ cup heavy whipping cream

¼ cup (½ stick) salted butter, melted and cooled slightly

2 large eggs, whisked

2 tablespoons chopped fresh chives, or 2 teaspoons dried

8 slices bacon, cooked and crumbled

1 cup shredded cheddar cheese

1. Preheat the oven to 350°F. Grease 10 wells of a standard-size muffin pan or line them with cupcake liners or silicone baking cups.

2. In a medium-size mixing bowl, whisk together the almond flour, sweetener, baking powder, and salt.

3. In a large mixing bowl, stir together the cream, cooled melted butter, eggs, and chives. Add the dry ingredients and stir until well combined. Gently fold in the bacon and cheese until completely combined.

4. Spoon the batter into the prepared wells of the muffin pan, filling them about three-quarters full. Bake for 20 to 25 minutes, until a toothpick inserted in the middle of a muffin comes out clean and the tops are light golden brown.

5. Allow to partially cool before removing from the pan. Best served fresh.

Note

Can be made the morning of the gathering, a few hours ahead of serving, and stored covered on the counter.

	NET CARBS 2.2g			
calories	fat	protein	carbs	fiber
285	26.4g	10.5g	4.2g	2g

Breakfast Enchiladas

yield 8 enchiladas (1 per serving) • *prep time* 20 minutes • *cook time* 25 minutes

6 large eggs

¼ cup heavy whipping cream

½ teaspoon ground cumin

¼ teaspoon salt

¼ teaspoon ground black pepper

1 pound bulk breakfast sausage

1 (4-ounce) can diced green chilies

½ cup shredded cheddar cheese

8 (8-inch) low-carb tortillas or egg wraps

1 cup salsa verde

1 cup shredded Monterey Jack cheese

Suggested garnishes:
Sliced black olives

Diced tomatoes

Sliced green onions

1. Preheat the oven to 350°F. Grease an 11 by 7-inch baking dish.

2. In a small mixing bowl, whisk together the eggs, cream, cumin, salt, and pepper.

3. In a medium-size skillet over medium heat, cook the sausage, crumbling the meat with a spatula, until browned, about 10 minutes. Stir in the green chilies.

4. Form a well in the center of the skillet. Pour the egg mixture into the well and let cook without stirring for 2 to 3 minutes, then gently stir the eggs until they are soft scrambled. Stir the eggs into the sausage mixture. Add the cheddar cheese and stir to combine.

5. To assemble the enchiladas, lay the tortillas side by side on the counter. Evenly fill the tortillas with the sausage mixture. Roll up the enchiladas and place them seam side down in the prepared baking dish.

6. Pour the salsa evenly over the enchiladas. Sprinkle evenly with the Monterey Jack cheese. Bake for 20 to 25 minutes, until the cheese has melted and is starting to turn light brown. Garnish with black olives, tomatoes, and/or green onions, if desired.

Note

I usually buy Mission Carb Balance tortillas in the soft taco size. The size in inches is not specified on the package.

NET CARBS 6.1g

calories	fat	protein	carbs	fiber
431	33.3g	23.4g	21.1g	15g

Brunch Parfaits

yield 6 servings • *prep time* 20 minutes • *cook time* 5 minutes

Granola:

2 tablespoons salted butter

½ cup raw pecan halves

⅓ cup unsweetened coconut flakes

¼ cup roasted and salted shelled sunflower seeds

2 tablespoons brown sugar substitute

1½ cups low-carb vanilla yogurt

1½ cups sliced strawberries

1 cup blueberries

1. Line a sheet pan with parchment paper.

2. To make the granola, melt the butter in a medium-size skillet over medium heat. Add the pecans, coconut flakes, sunflower seeds, and brown sugar substitute and stir to coat in the melted butter. Cook, stirring occasionally, until fragrant and toasted, 3 to 5 minutes. Spread the granola evenly on the sheet pan. Allow to cool completely.

3. Layer 2 tablespoons of yogurt in the bottoms of six 8-ounce wide-mouth jars or cups. Add a sprinkle of the granola to each jar followed by 2 tablespoons of sliced strawberries and a heaping tablespoon of blueberries. Repeat the layers once more. Cover and refrigerate until ready to serve.

Make Ahead

Can be made up to 1 day ahead. Store covered in the refrigerator.

	NET CARBS	3.6g		
calories	fat	protein	carbs	fiber
209	15.5g	12g	5.9g	2.3g

Home Fries

yield 6 servings • *prep time* 10 minutes • *cook time* 25 minutes

3 tablespoons bacon drippings

¼ cup chopped onions

8 ounces radishes, diced

8 ounces turnips, diced

½ teaspoon paprika

¼ teaspoon salt

¼ teaspoon ground black pepper

Chopped fresh parsley, for garnish (optional)

1. Melt the bacon drippings in a large skillet over medium heat. Add the onions and cook until tender, about 5 minutes.

2. Put the radishes and turnips in the skillet and cook over medium-high heat for 10 minutes, then reduce the heat to medium. Add the paprika, salt, and pepper. Continue cooking for 10 to 15 more minutes, stirring every couple of minutes, until the radishes and turnips are fork-tender and slightly crispy and caramelized around the edges.

3. Garnish with parsley, if desired, and serve immediately.

Note ——————————————

Ghee or avocado oil can be used in place of the bacon drippings, although the drippings add a nice depth of flavor to this dish.

NET CARBS 2.9g

calories	fat	protein	carbs	fiber
87	7.6g	0.7g	4.3g	1.4g

Andouille Sausage Sheet Pan Breakfast

yield 6 servings • *prep time* 10 minutes • *cook time* 30 to 35 minutes

2 tablespoons avocado oil

½ teaspoon smoked paprika

¼ teaspoon garlic powder

¼ teaspoon salt

¼ teaspoon ground black pepper

1 pound radishes, diced

12 ounces andouille sausage, sliced

6 large eggs

Chopped fresh parsley, for garnish

1. Preheat the oven to 425°F.

2. In a medium-size mixing bowl, whisk together the oil, smoked paprika, garlic powder, salt, and pepper. Add the radishes and sausage to the bowl and stir to coat in the oil.

3. Spread the radishes and sausage evenly on a sheet pan. Roast for 25 minutes, or until the radishes are tender and browned around the edges and the sausage is browned.

4. Create 6 wells in the radish and sausage mixture. Carefully crack an egg into each well. Return the pan to the oven and bake for 5 to 7 more minutes, until the whites are set and the yolks are still runny. (If you prefer more done yolks, increase the baking time accordingly.) Garnish with parsley before serving.

NET CARBS 1.9g

calories	fat	protein	carbs	fiber
246	19.5g	14.9g	3.2g	1.3g

Sheet Pan Buttermilk Pancakes

yield 8 servings (2 squares per serving) • *prep time* 10 minutes • *cook time* 20 minutes

2 cups finely ground blanched almond flour

¼ cup coconut flour

¼ teaspoon granular sweetener

1 tablespoon baking powder

½ teaspoon salt

1 cup unsweetened almond milk

1 tablespoon white vinegar

5 large eggs

4 tablespoons (½ stick) salted butter, melted and cooled slightly, plus more for serving if desired

1 teaspoon pure vanilla extract

½ cup berries of choice

Sugar-free maple syrup, for serving (optional)

1. Preheat the oven to 425°F. Grease a sheet pan with oil.

2. In a medium-size mixing bowl, whisk together the almond flour, coconut flour, sweetener, baking powder, and salt.

3. In a small mixing bowl, mix together the almond milk and vinegar. Let sit for 5 minutes.

4. In a second small mixing bowl, whisk together the eggs and cooled melted butter. Stir the egg mixture into the flour mixture until combined. Stir in the milk mixture a little at a time until all of the ingredients are incorporated. Stir in the vanilla.

5. Spread the batter evenly on the prepared sheet pan. Top with the berries and bake for 15 to 20 minutes, until light golden brown. Run a knife around the edge before cutting into 16 squares. Serve with butter and sugar-free maple syrup, if desired.

Note

I created this recipe for my family because we all like pancakes, and it can be hard to serve fresh pancakes to everyone at once. This recipe solves that problem, giving you more time to focus on important things, like cooking the bacon to go with it!

NET CARBS 4.3g

calories	fat	protein	carbs	fiber
270	22.9g	10.3g	7.8g	3.5g

Pecan Pie Muffins

yield 9 muffins (1 muffin per serving) • *prep time* 10 minutes • *cook time* 30 minutes

½ cup finely ground blanched almond flour

1 tablespoon coconut flour

¾ cup brown sugar substitute

1 cup chopped raw pecans, plus 9 pecan halves for topping

2 large eggs

½ cup salted butter, melted and cooled slightly

½ teaspoon pure vanilla extract

1. Preheat the oven to 325°F. Line 9 wells of a standard-size muffin pan with cupcake liners or silicone baking cups.

2. In a medium-size mixing bowl, combine the almond flour, coconut flour, brown sugar substitute, and chopped pecans. In a small mixing bowl, whisk together the eggs, cooled melted butter, and vanilla.

3. Pour the egg mixture into the flour mixture and stir until the wet and dry ingredients are incorporated.

4. Spoon the batter into the prepared wells of the muffin pan, filling them nearly to the top. Place a pecan half on top of each muffin.

5. Bake for 25 to 30 minutes, until a toothpick inserted in the center of a muffin comes out clean. Allow to cool for 10 minutes before removing from the pan. Because of their ooey gooey pecan pie–like center, these muffins are best served warm.

Make Ahead

These muffins are best served fresh; however, they can be made up to 1 day ahead. Store in an airtight container in the refrigerator. When ready to serve, reheat in the microwave on high for a few seconds. Reheating is needed to obtain the pecan pie filling texture.

NET CARBS 1.2g

calories	fat	protein	carbs	fiber
238	23.7g	4.3g	3.3g	2.1g

Glazed Cinnamon Biscuits

yield 8 biscuits (1 per serving) • *prep time* 10 minutes • *cook time* 12 minutes

1½ cups finely ground blanched almond flour

½ cup granular sweetener

2 teaspoons baking powder

1 teaspoon ground cinnamon

¼ teaspoon salt

¼ cup sour cream

2 large eggs, whisked

2 tablespoons salted butter, melted and slightly cooled

Vanilla glaze:

¼ cup confectioners' sweetener

¼ cup heavy whipping cream

½ teaspoon pure vanilla extract

Pinch of salt

1. Preheat the oven to 400°F. Line a baking sheet with parchment paper.

2. In a medium-size mixing bowl, whisk together the almond flour, granular sweetener, baking powder, cinnamon, and salt.

3. In a small mixing bowl, whisk together the sour cream, eggs, and cooled melted butter. Pour the sour cream mixture into the dry ingredients and stir until well combined. Allow to sit for 5 minutes.

4. Use a 2-ounce cookie scoop or ice cream scoop to drop the batter onto the prepared baking sheet, leaving about 2 inches between the biscuits. Bake for 12 to 14 minutes, until the tops are golden brown.

5. While the biscuits are baking, prepare the glaze: In a small mixing bowl, stir together the confectioners' sweetener, cream, vanilla, and salt.

6. Remove the biscuits from the oven and allow to cool for 10 minutes. Drizzle the glaze over the biscuits while still warm. Serve immediately.

Note

This sweeter-style biscuit was inspired by my mom's biscuits, which almost always include some cinnamon and sweetener. The glaze is a nice touch when entertaining, but you could certainly omit it and eat them warm with a pat of butter. If you're looking for a savory low-carb biscuit to add to a brunch buffet, I recommend the recipe for drop biscuits in my first book, Southern Keto.

NET CARBS 2.4g

calories	fat	protein	carbs	fiber
193	17.7g	5.9g	4.4g	2g

Appetizers & Bites

Nashville Hot Peanuts

yield 2 cups (¼ cup per serving) • *prep time* 5 minutes • *cook time* 25 minutes

2 cups unsalted dry roasted peanuts

2 tablespoons avocado oil

1 tablespoon brown sugar substitute

½ teaspoon salt

½ teaspoon ground black pepper

½ teaspoon cayenne pepper

½ teaspoon smoked paprika

1. Preheat the oven to 325°F. Line a sheet pan with parchment paper.

2. Place the peanuts in a medium-size mixing bowl.

3. Put the oil, brown sugar substitute, salt, black pepper, cayenne pepper, and smoked paprika in a small mixing bowl and stir to combine. Pour the oil mixture over the peanuts and gently toss until all of the peanuts are coated.

4. Spread the peanuts evenly on the prepared pan. Bake, stirring every 5 minutes, until lightly browned, 20 to 25 minutes. Let cool on the pan before serving. The flavors will develop further as the peanuts cool.

Notes

Nashville hot chicken is all the rage. It was made famous in Nashville, Tennessee, but its popularity has extended well beyond that city's borders. I included a hot chicken recipe in Southern Keto: Beyond the Basics *and was inspired to use the same flavors in these nuts.*

The amount of cayenne pepper called for here will create moderately hot peanuts. If you want more heat, use more cayenne.

Make Ahead

Can be made up to 1 week ahead. Store in an airtight container at room temperature.

	NET CARBS 3.8g			
calories	fat	protein	carbs	fiber
198	17.6g	7g	6.3g	2.5g

Crab Rangoon–Stuffed Mushrooms

yield 16 mushrooms (2 mushrooms per serving) • *prep time* 15 minutes • *cook time* 25 minutes

16 medium white mushrooms (about 8 ounces)

Filling:

4 ounces cream cheese (½ cup), softened

1 green onion, sliced, plus more for garnish if desired

1 clove garlic, minced

2 teaspoons Worcestershire sauce

1 teaspoon coconut aminos

½ teaspoon ground black pepper

8 ounces lump crab meat

1. Preheat the oven to 375°F. Line a sheet pan with parchment paper.

2. Clean the mushrooms and pat them dry. Remove and discard the stems. Set the mushroom caps cavity side up on the prepared pan.

3. To make the filling, put the cream cheese, green onion, garlic, Worcestershire sauce, aminos, and pepper in a medium-size mixing bowl and stir until well combined. Fold in the crab meat.

4. Fill each mushroom with a spoonful of the crab mixture and return the stuffed mushrooms to the pan.

5. Bake until the filling is hot, bubbly, and lightly browned, 20 to 25 minutes. Garnish with sliced green onions, if desired.

Make Ahead

The filling can be made up to 1 day ahead. On the day of the event, follow the rest of the recipe as directed.

NET CARBS 1.4g

calories	fat	protein	carbs	fiber
80	5.2g	6.9g	1.9g	0.5g

Baked Jalapeño Pimento Cheese Dip

yield 8 servings • *prep time* 10 minutes • *cook time* 25 minutes

2 cups shredded sharp cheddar cheese

4 ounces cream cheese (½ cup), softened

½ cup mayonnaise

½ cup sour cream

1 (4-ounce) can pimentos, drained

1 jalapeño pepper, seeded and finely chopped

½ teaspoon smoked paprika

½ teaspoon ground black pepper

¼ teaspoon garlic powder

¼ teaspoon salt

Chopped fresh parsley, for garnish (optional)

Serving suggestions:

Pork rinds, mini sweet peppers or bell pepper strips, cucumber rounds, celery sticks, and/or low-carb crackers

1. Preheat the oven to 375°F. Grease a 9-inch round baking dish with oil.

2. Put all of the ingredients in a large mixing bowl and stir until well combined.

3. Spread the dip evenly in the prepared baking dish. Bake for 20 to 25 minutes, until bubbling around the edges and browned on top.

4. Allow to cool for 10 minutes before serving. Garnish with parsley, if desired, and serve with the scoopers of your choice.

Note

Freshly shredded cheddar cheese will give you the best results for this dip.

Make Ahead

You can combine the ingredients the day before serving. Spread the dip in the prepared baking dish and bake it on the day of the event.

	NET CARBS 1.8g			
calories	fat	protein	carbs	fiber
268	26.4g	7g	2.3g	0.4g

Caramelized Onion Dip

yield 8 servings • *prep time* 10 minutes, plus 2 hours to chill • *cook time* 20 minutes

2 tablespoons salted butter

1 large onion, thinly sliced

1 cup sour cream

¼ cup mayonnaise

1 tablespoon chopped fresh parsley

1 teaspoon Worcestershire sauce

½ teaspoon garlic powder

½ teaspoon salt

½ teaspoon ground black pepper

Fresh parsley leaves, for garnish (optional)

Serving suggestions:

Pork rinds, mini sweet peppers or bell pepper strips, cucumber rounds, celery sticks, Parmesan crisps, and/or low-carb crackers

1. Melt the butter in a medium-size skillet over medium heat. Add the onion and cook until caramelized, about 20 minutes, stirring every few minutes. Toward the end of cooking, stir the onion slices every minute or so to prevent burning. If the slices begin to stick to the pan, add a few drops of water. When done, they will be golden brown and very soft.

2. In a medium-size mixing bowl, stir together the sour cream, mayonnaise, parsley, Worcestershire sauce, garlic powder, salt, and pepper. Fold in the onions until well combined.

3. Transfer the dip to a serving bowl and refrigerate for at least 2 hours. The longer the dip chills, the more the flavors will develop. Garnish with parsley, if desired, and serve with the scoopers of your choice.

Make Ahead

Can be made up to 2 days ahead. Store in an airtight container in the refrigerator.

NET CARBS 2.2g

calories	fat	protein	carbs	fiber
139	13.6g	1.2g	2.5g	0.4g

Crispy Crackers

yield 6 servings • *prep time* 10 minutes • *cook time* 15 minutes

1 cup finely ground blanched almond flour

¼ cup whey protein powder (unflavored and unsweetened)

¼ teaspoon baking powder

1 large egg white

1 tablespoon salted butter, melted and cooled slightly

1 tablespoon water, plus more if needed

Toasted sesame seeds, for topping (optional)

Note ———

The crackers are easily customizable. Simply add your choice of dry seasonings, such as dried chives or everything bagel seasoning, to the dough.

1. Preheat the oven to 350°F. Have on hand a baking sheet.

2. In a medium-size mixing bowl, whisk together the almond flour, whey protein, and baking powder.

3. In a small mixing bowl, whisk together the egg white, cooled melted butter, and water. Add the egg white mixture to the flour mixture and stir until a cohesive dough forms. If the dough is too dry, add more water 1 teaspoon at a time until it holds together.

4. Place the dough on a piece of parchment paper the same size as your baking sheet. Top it with another equal-sized piece of parchment and use a rolling pin to roll out the dough into a rectangle about ⅛ inch thick.

5. Remove the top piece of parchment paper and use a pizza cutter to cut the dough into 2-inch square crackers. Spread them about 1 inch apart, then carefully slide the parchment with the crackers onto the baking sheet. Sprinkle with toasted sesame seeds, if desired.

6. Bake for 12 to 15 minutes, until the crackers start to brown around the edges. Allow to cool completely on the pan before removing. They will crisp up as they cool.

Note ———

If doubling this recipe, divide the dough into two equal portions after completing Step 3, then follow the recipe as written using two baking sheets.

Make Ahead ———

Can be made up to 3 days ahead. Store in an airtight container at room temperature.

NET CARBS 1.4g

calories	fat	protein	carbs	fiber
151	11.9g	8.9g	3.4g	2g

Shrimp Cocktail Cups

yield 12 servings • *prep time* 10 minutes

Cocktail sauce:

1 cup ketchup (no sugar added)

2 teaspoons prepared horseradish

2 teaspoons Worcestershire sauce

1 teaspoon freshly squeezed lemon juice

36 large cooked shrimp, preferably tail on

12 small lemon wedges, for serving

Fresh parsley, for garnish (optional)

Special equipment: **12 (8-ounce) clear serving cups**

1. To make the cocktail sauce, stir together the ketchup, horseradish, Worcestershire sauce, and lemon juice in a small mixing bowl until well combined.

2. To assemble the cups, divide the cocktail sauce evenly among the serving cups. Arrange 3 shrimp along the rim of each cup. Serve with lemon wedges and garnish with parsley, if desired. Best served the same day.

Make Ahead

The cocktail sauce can be made up to 3 days ahead. Store in an airtight jar in the refrigerator.

NET CARBS 1.8g

calories	fat	protein	carbs	fiber
53	0.6g	8g	1.8g	0g

Caesar Salad Parfaits

yield 8 servings • *prep time* 15 minutes • *cook time* 10 minutes

1 cup shredded Parmesan cheese, for the crisps

Caesar dressing:

1 cup mayonnaise

½ cup grated Parmesan cheese

2 tablespoons freshly squeezed lemon juice

1 clove garlic, minced

1 teaspoon anchovy paste

1 teaspoon Dijon mustard

1 teaspoon Worcestershire sauce

¼ teaspoon freshly ground black pepper

¼ teaspoon salt

4 cups chopped romaine lettuce

1 cup shaved Parmesan cheese

Special equipment: 8 (8-ounce) clear serving cups

1. To make the Parmesan crisps, line a microwave-safe plate with parchment paper. Divide the shredded Parmesan cheese evenly into 8 small piles onto the parchment, spacing them 2 inches apart. Microwave on high for 1 minute 30 seconds, or until the crisps are starting to brown. Slide the sheet of parchment paper with the crisps onto another plate. Allow to cool before removing the crisps from the parchment.

2. To make the dressing, put all of the dressing ingredients in a small mixing bowl and whisk until well combined.

3. Divide the lettuce evenly among the serving cups, putting about ½ cup of lettuce in each one. Top each lettuce cup with 2 generous tablespoons of dressing. Evenly sprinkle the shaved Parmesan on top of the salad cups. Garnish with the Parmesan crisps. Best served immediately but can be eaten later the same day.

Make Ahead

The dressing can be made up to 1 day ahead. The Parmesan crisps can be made the morning of the gathering.

	NET CARBS 0.6g			
calories	fat	protein	carbs	fiber
324	30.9g	11.9g	1.2g	0.6g

Mini Salami Cheese Balls

yield 8 mini cheese balls (1 per serving) • *prep time* 15 minutes, plus 2 hours to chill

1 (8-ounce) package cream cheese, softened

4 ounces hard salami, finely chopped

1 green onion, sliced

¼ cup finely chopped raw pecans

Serving suggestions:
Pork rinds, Parmesan crisps, and/or low-carb crackers

Special equipment: **Cocktail toothpicks**

1. In a medium-size mixing bowl, stir together the cream cheese, salami, and green onion until well blended.

2. Shape the mixture into eight 1-inch balls. Roll each ball in the pecans and insert a cocktail toothpick in the top. Place on a serving plate, cover, and refrigerate for at least 2 hours before serving.

Make Ahead
Can be made up to 1 day ahead. Store in an airtight container in the refrigerator.

	NET CARBS 1.4g			
calories	fat	protein	carbs	fiber
208	19.8g	5.8g	2.2g	0.8g

Savory Party Snack Mix

yield 4 cups (½ cup per serving) • *prep time* 5 minutes • *cook time* 1 hour

½ cup (1 stick) salted butter, melted

3 tablespoons Worcestershire sauce

1½ teaspoons seasoned salt

1 teaspoon garlic powder

1 teaspoon onion powder

4 cups bite-size pork rind pieces

1 cup unsalted dry-roasted almonds

1 cup unsalted dry-roasted peanuts

1 cup Parmesan crisps

1. Preheat the oven to 250°F. Line a sheet pan with parchment paper.

2. In a small mixing bowl, stir together the melted butter, Worcestershire sauce, seasoned salt, garlic powder, and onion powder until well combined.

3. Place the pork rinds, almonds, peanuts, and Parmesan crisps in a large mixing bowl. Lightly toss with a rubber spatula to combine. Pour the butter mixture over the pork rind mixture and gently toss again until all of the pieces are coated.

4. Spread the mixture evenly on the prepared pan. Bake for 1 hour, stirring every 15 minutes, until lightly browned and crispy. Let cool on the pan before serving. The flavors will develop further as the snack mix cools.

Note

This low-carb alternative to traditional snack mix has all the delicious flavors of the savory snack mix you know and love, better known as Chex Mix.

Make Ahead

Can be made up to 3 days ahead. Store in an airtight container at room temperature.

NET CARBS 4.4g

calories	fat	protein	carbs	fiber
366	32.5g	14.8g	7.5g	3.1g

Blender Salsa

yield 4 cups (¼ cup per serving) • *prep time* 10 minutes

1 (28-ounce) can petite diced tomatoes

1 jalapeño pepper, seeded

½ medium onion, quartered

¼ cup chopped fresh cilantro

2 cloves garlic, peeled

Juice of 1 lime

2 teaspoons ground cumin

1 teaspoon salt

½ teaspoon granular sweetener

Serving suggestions:
Pork rinds, mini sweet peppers or bell pepper strips, cucumber rounds, celery sticks, Parmesan crisps, and/or low-carb tortilla chips

In the order listed, place all of the ingredients in a blender. Pulse until the salsa reaches the desired consistency; I like it slightly chunky. Serve with the scoopers of your choice.

Make Ahead

Can be made up to 3 days ahead. Store in an airtight jar in the refrigerator.

NET CARBS 2.1g

calories	fat	protein	carbs	fiber
13	0.1g	0.6g	2.8g	0.6g

Creamy Spicy Corn Dip

yield 8 servings • *prep time* 10 minutes • *cook time* 25 minutes

1 (8-ounce) package cream cheese, softened

1 cup sour cream

½ cup mayonnaise

1 (15-ounce) can baby corn, drained and chopped

1 red bell pepper, diced

1 green onion, sliced

1 jalapeño pepper, seeded and finely chopped

1 teaspoon chili powder

1 teaspoon ground cumin

1 teaspoon sweet corn extract

Chopped fresh cilantro or parsley, for garnish (optional)

Serving suggestions:

Pork rinds, mini sweet peppers or bell pepper strips, cucumber rounds, celery sticks, and/or low-carb tortilla chips or crackers

1. Preheat the oven to 375°F. Grease an 11 by 7-inch baking dish with oil.

2. In a medium-size mixing bowl, stir together the cream cheese, sour cream, and mayonnaise until thoroughly combined. Add the corn, bell pepper, green onion, jalapeño, chili powder, cumin, and corn extract and stir until well combined.

3. Spread the mixture evenly in the prepared baking dish. Bake for 20 to 25 minutes, until the dip is lightly browned on top and bubbling around the edges. Allow to cool slightly, then garnish with cilantro or parsley, if desired. Serve with the scoopers of your choice.

Notes

My family loves dips with corn in them, but corn is high in carbohydrates. Simply switching to baby corn lowers the carb count by a lot. Though baby corn isn't quite as sweet as yellow corn, it makes a delicious substitute when combined with corn extract.

I buy corn extract on Amazon.com. Looking for other uses for it? See the recipes for Jalapeño Corn Dog Poppers (page 162) and Sausage Corn Chowder (page 202). Also, you might try my Skillet Cornbread recipe in Southern Keto *or the Corn Dog Casserole in* Southern Keto: Beyond the Basics.

Make Ahead

Can be made up to 1 day ahead. Complete Step 2 and store the mixture in an airtight container in the refrigerator. The day of the gathering, complete Steps 1 and 3, spreading the dip in the prepared baking dish and baking it immediately before serving.

NET CARBS 2.8g

calories	fat	protein	carbs	fiber
277	26.9g	3.8g	4.5g	1.6g

Restaurant-Style Queso Dip

yield 10 servings • *prep time* 5 minutes • *cook time* 15 minutes

1 pound deli white American cheese, cut into chunks

½ cup heavy whipping cream

½ cup unsweetened almond milk

1 tablespoon salted butter

2 (4-ounce) cans chopped green chilies

1 jalapeño pepper, seeded and finely chopped

¼ teaspoon ground cumin

¼ teaspoon salt

Serving suggestions:
Low-carb tortilla chips, pork rinds, mini sweet peppers or bell pepper strips, cucumber rounds, celery sticks, and/or Parmesan crisps

1. Heat the cheese, cream, almond milk, and butter in a medium-size saucepan over low heat, stirring frequently, until the cheese has melted, about 15 minutes.

2. Stir in the green chilies, jalapeño, cumin, and salt and serve with the scoopers of your choice.

Notes

You can usually find white American cheese at the deli counter in supermarkets.

You can also make this dip in a slow cooker. Simply cook it on low until the cheese mixture is melted, then stir and turn to the warm setting.

NET CARBS 0.9g

calories	fat	protein	carbs	fiber
223	20.5g	8.8g	1g	0.1g

Fiesta Layered Dip Cups

yield 8 servings • *prep time* 15 minutes (not including time to make seasoning, guacamole, and salsa)

1 cup sour cream

2 tablespoons Taco Seasoning (page 300)

1 cup Large Batch Guacamole (page 142)

1 cup Blender Salsa (page 132)

1 cup shredded cheddar cheese

1 (4-ounce) can sliced black olives

2 green onions, sliced

Serving suggestions:
Pork rinds, mini sweet peppers or bell pepper strips, cucumber rounds, celery sticks, and/or low-carb tortilla chips or crackers

Special equipment: 8 (8-ounce) clear serving cups

1. In a small mixing bowl, mix together the sour cream and taco seasoning.

2. To assemble the cups, layer the ingredients in each serving cup in this order: 2 tablespoons of guacamole, 2 tablespoons of seasoned sour cream, 2 tablespoons of salsa, 2 tablespoons of cheese, 4 or 5 black olive slices, and a sprinkling of green onion slices. Cover the cups and store in the refrigerator until ready to serve.

3. The dip cups are best eaten the same day or the next day at the latest. Serve with the scoopers of your choice.

Make Ahead

The salsa can be made up to 3 days before assembly, and the sour cream mixture up to 1 day before.

NET CARBS 2.8g

calories	fat	protein	carbs	fiber
148	12.1g	4.4g	4.6g	1.8g

Cheesy Hot Crab Dip

yield 8 servings • *prep time* 10 minutes • *cook time* 25 minutes

4 ounces cream cheese (½ cup), softened

¼ cup mayonnaise

¼ cup sour cream

2 green onions, sliced, plus more for garnish if desired

1 teaspoon Old Bay seasoning

½ teaspoon Worcestershire sauce

½ teaspoon salt

8 ounces lump crab meat

1 cup shredded cheddar cheese, divided

Serving suggestions:

Pork rinds, mini sweet peppers or bell pepper strips, cucumber rounds, celery sticks, and/or low-carb crackers or tortilla chips

1. Preheat the oven to 350°F. Grease a 2-quart baking dish with oil.

2. In a medium-size mixing bowl, stir together the cream cheese, mayonnaise, sour cream, green onions, Old Bay seasoning, Worcestershire sauce, and salt until well combined. Gently fold in the crab meat and ½ cup of the cheddar cheese.

3. Spread the dip evenly in the prepared baking dish. Top with the remaining ½ cup of cheese. Bake for 20 to 25 minutes, until the dip is lightly browned on top and bubbling around the edges.

4. Let cool for 10 minutes before serving. Garnish with sliced green onions, if desired. Serve with the scoopers of your choice.

Make Ahead

Can be made up to 1 day ahead. Complete Step 2 and store the dip in an airtight container in the refrigerator. The day of the gathering, complete Steps 1, 3, and 4.

NET CARBS 1.1g

calories	fat	protein	carbs	fiber
193	16.9g	9.3g	1.2g	0.1g

Large Batch Guacamole

yield 3 cups (¼ cup per serving) • *prep time* 10 minutes

5 ripe Hass avocados, peeled and pitted

½ medium red onion, chopped

2 Roma tomatoes, diced

2 cloves garlic, minced

Juice of 1 lime

¼ cup chopped fresh cilantro

1 jalapeño pepper, seeded and finely chopped

½ teaspoon salt

¼ teaspoon ground black pepper

Serving suggestions:
Pork rinds, mini sweet peppers or bell pepper strips, cucumber rounds, celery sticks, and/or low-carb tortilla chips or crackers

1. Put the avocados in a medium-size serving bowl and use a fork to mash them to the desired consistency. Stir in the rest of the ingredients until well combined. Taste and add more salt and pepper, if desired.

2. Serve immediately with the scoopers of your choice.

Note

To avoid unsightly browning, guacamole should be made the same day it will be served, ideally as close to serving time as possible. If necessary, store it in the refrigerator with plastic wrap pressed directly on the surface of the guacamole to minimize oxidation.

NET CARBS 2.2g

calories	fat	protein	carbs	fiber
106	9.2g	1.5g	6.7g	4.5g

Pretzel Bites & Cheese Sauce

yield 8 servings • *prep time* 15 minutes (not including time to make dough) • *cook time* 20 minutes

1 recipe Multi-Purpose Dough (page 306)

1 large egg yolk, whisked

Coarse salt

Cheese sauce:

¾ cup heavy whipping cream

2 tablespoons salted butter

1 cup shredded cheddar cheese

½ teaspoon ground mustard

¼ teaspoon salt

1. Preheat the oven to 400°F. Line a sheet pan with parchment paper.

2. Place the dough on a silicone mat or piece of parchment paper. Divide the dough into four equal parts, then roll each section into a rope about 1 inch thick. Cut each rope into ¾-inch pieces. Place the pieces on the prepared pan.

3. Brush the pretzel bites with the whisked egg yolk and sprinkle them with coarse salt.

4. Bake for 12 to 15 minutes, until the tops are golden brown.

5. Meanwhile, prepare the cheese sauce: Heat the cream and butter in a medium-size saucepan over low heat. When the butter has melted, stir in the cheese, mustard, and salt. Continue to stir until the cheese has melted and the sauce is smooth, about 10 minutes.

6. Serve the pretzel bites with the cheese sauce. The bites are best eaten the same day; the sauce should be enjoyed while still warm.

NET CARBS 2g

calories	fat	protein	carbs	fiber
282	26.9g	10g	3.2g	1.1g

Praline Pecan Brie

yield 8 servings • *prep time* 15 minutes • *cook time* 20 minutes

1 (8-ounce) wheel Brie cheese

½ cup raw pecan halves, chopped

¼ cup (½ stick) salted butter

2 tablespoons brown sugar substitute

1 tablespoon sugar-free maple syrup

Pinch of salt

Fresh rosemary sprigs, for garnish

Serving suggestions:
Parmesan crisps and/or low-carb crackers

1. Preheat the oven to 350°F. Line a sheet pan with parchment paper.

2. Place the Brie on the prepared pan and gently score the top of the rind with a knife (don't cut too deep). Bake for 12 minutes, until the cheese is just starting to melt.

3. Meanwhile, prepare the praline pecan mixture: In a medium-size skillet over medium heat, toast the pecans for 3 to 4 minutes, stirring often. Remove the nuts from the skillet and set aside.

4. In the same skillet still over medium heat, warm the butter, brown sugar substitute, and maple syrup, stirring until everything has melted and is well combined. Stir the pecans and pinch of salt into the mixture and remove the pan from the heat.

5. Transfer the Brie to a serving plate and pour the praline pecan mixture over the cheese. Garnish with rosemary sprigs and serve immediately with the scoopers of your choice.

NET CARBS 0.3g

calories	fat	protein	carbs	fiber
205	20.1g	4.9g	1g	0.8g

Jalapeño Popper Cheese Ball

yield 12 servings • *prep time* 15 minutes, plus 2 hours to chill

2 (8-ounce) packages cream cheese, softened

6 slices bacon, cooked and crumbled

1 cup shredded cheddar cheese

2 jalapeño peppers, seeded and finely chopped

1 green onion, sliced

½ teaspoon garlic powder

¼ teaspoon salt

¼ teaspoon ground black pepper

½ cup finely chopped raw pecans

Serving suggestions:

Pork rinds, mini sweet peppers or bell pepper strips, cucumber rounds, celery sticks, Parmesan crisps, and/or low-carb crackers

1. In a medium-size mixing bowl, stir together the cream cheese, bacon, cheddar cheese, jalapeños, green onion, garlic powder, salt, and pepper until well combined.

2. Shape the mixture into a ball and roll it in the pecans. Wrap the ball in plastic wrap and refrigerate for at least 2 hours. Serve with the scoopers of your choice.

Make Ahead

Can be made up to 3 days ahead. Store in an airtight container in the refrigerator.

	NET CARBS 1.2g			
calories	fat	protein	carbs	fiber
226	21.5g	6.8g	1.8g	0.6g

Pepperoni Pizza Bites

yield 24 bites (2 per serving) • *prep time* 5 minutes • *cook time* 10 minutes

24 slices deli-cut pepperoni, about ¹⁄₁₆ inch thick

¼ cup low-sugar marinara sauce

1 cup shredded mozzarella cheese

Italian seasoning, for garnish

Special equipment: **24-well mini muffin pan**

1. Preheat the oven to 400°F.

2. Make four evenly spaced ¼-inch cuts in each pepperoni slice, leaving the center intact. Place a slice in each well of a 24-well mini muffin pan, pressing it firmly into the bottom and allowing the sides to overlap. Bake for 5 minutes.

3. Spoon ½ teaspoon of the sauce and 2 teaspoons of the mozzarella into each pepperoni bite. Sprinkle the bites with Italian seasoning and bake for 3 to 5 more minutes, until the cheese has melted. Let cool for 10 minutes, then use a small spatula to remove the bites from the pan. Best served immediately.

Note

I like to buy the pepperoni for this recipe freshly sliced from the deli because I can get slices that are a little thicker than packaged presliced pepperoni. Thinner slices would work but would be more fragile.

NET CARBS 0.8g

calories	fat	protein	carbs	fiber
80	6.5g	4.5g	0.8g	0.1g

Bacon Jalapeño Deviled Eggs

yield 12 deviled eggs (2 per serving) • *prep time* 20 minutes • *cook time* 15 minutes

6 large eggs

⅓ cup mayonnaise

1 clove garlic, minced

1 teaspoon ground mustard

¼ teaspoon salt

¼ teaspoon ground black pepper

6 slices bacon, cooked and finely diced, plus cooked bacon pieces for garnish if desired

1 jalapeño pepper, seeded and finely chopped

Paprika, for garnish

1. Place the eggs in a single layer in a medium-size saucepan. Cover with water by 3 inches. Bring to a boil over high heat. Cover the pan and remove from the heat. Let the eggs sit in the hot water for 15 minutes.

2. Rinse the eggs with cold water until cool. Crack the shells and gently peel the eggs under cold running water. Slice the eggs in half lengthwise, then carefully remove the yolks and place them in a medium-size mixing bowl.

3. Add the mayonnaise to the bowl with the yolks and use a fork to mash the yolks and mayonnaise until smooth. Stir in the garlic, ground mustard, salt, and pepper. Fold in the bacon and jalapeño until well combined.

4. Spoon the yolk mixture into the egg white halves and garnish with paprika and extra bacon pieces, if desired.

Note

This recipe can be double or even tripled. Just make sure to use a pan large enough to fit the eggs in single layer. If needed, cook the eggs in batches.

Make Ahead

The deviled eggs can be made up to 2 days ahead; the eggs can be hard-boiled up to 4 days in advance.

NET CARBS 0.7g

calories	fat	protein	carbs	fiber
218	20.1g	9.9g	0.8g	0.1g

Olive Pinwheels

yield 36 pinwheels (2 per serving) • *prep time* 15 minutes (not including time to make seasoning), plus 2 hours to chill

1 (8-ounce) package cream cheese, softened

1 (4-ounce) can diced green chilies

1 (4-ounce) can chopped black olives, drained

2 tablespoons Ranch Seasoning (page 301)

1 teaspoon ground cumin

1 cup shredded Mexican cheese blend

6 (8-inch) low-carb flour tortillas

1. In a medium-size mixing bowl, stir together the cream cheese, green chilies, olives, ranch seasoning, and cumin until thoroughly mixed. Fold in the shredded cheese until well combined.

2. Spoon about 3 tablespoons of the cream cheese mixture onto each tortilla. Use a small spatula to spread the filling, leaving a ¼-inch border all around. Roll each tortilla tightly and wrap individually in plastic wrap. Refrigerate for at least 2 hours to allow the flavors to develop.

3. To serve, slice each tortilla roll into 6 pieces.

Make Ahead ——————

Can be made up to 1 day ahead. Store in an airtight container in the refrigerator.

NET CARBS 2.1g

calories	fat	protein	carbs	fiber
104	8.5g	4g	7.3g	5.1g

Smoked Salmon Bites with Dill Cream Cheese

yield 20 bites (2 per serving) • *prep time* 10 minutes

4 ounces cream cheese (½ cup), softened

2 tablespoons chopped fresh dill, plus 20 small sprigs for garnish

1 tablespoon finely diced red onion

¼ teaspoon salt

¼ teaspoon ground black pepper

20 (¼-inch-thick) slices English cucumber (about ½ cucumber, depending on size)

2 ounces smoked salmon, cut into 20 (1-inch) pieces

1. In a small mixing bowl, stir together the cream cheese, chopped dill, onion, salt, and pepper until well combined.

2. Top each cucumber slice with about 1 teaspoon of the cream cheese mixture, followed by a piece of smoked salmon. Garnish with a small sprig of dill. Refrigerate for up to 2 hours before serving.

Make Ahead

The cream cheese mixture can be made up to 1 day ahead. Store in an airtight container in the refrigerator.

NET CARBS 1.2g

calories	fat	protein	carbs	fiber
53	4.3g	2.1g	1.4g	0.2g

Antipasto Skewers

yield 12 skewers (2 per serving) • *prep time* 15 minutes

12 grape or cherry tomatoes

12 marinated artichoke heart quarters

12 marinated fresh mini mozzarella balls

12 slices salami

12 fresh basil leaves

12 pitted black olives

Special equipment: **12 cocktail picks**

Thread one of each ingredient onto each cocktail pick. Arrange the skewers on a serving platter or on small plates and serve. Best eaten the same day.

Note

This recipe is easily customizable using a variety of meats, cheeses, and vegetables.

NET CARBS 1.9g

calories	fat	protein	carbs	fiber
130	8.6g	9.6g	4.2g	2.3g

Everything Bagel Pigs in a Blanket

yield 12 servings (2 per serving) • *prep time* 15 minutes • *cook time* 15 minutes

2 (8-inch) low-carb flour tortillas

2 ounces cream cheese (¼ cup), softened

2 teaspoons everything bagel seasoning, plus more for garnish

24 beef cocktail smoked sausages (about 8 ounces)

1 tablespoon salted butter, melted

Special equipment: **Cocktail toothpicks, for serving**

1. Preheat the oven to 400°F. Line a sheet pan with parchment paper.

2. Divide the cream cheese evenly between the tortillas, spreading it across the surface and to the edges.

3. Sprinkle each tortilla with 1 teaspoon of everything bagel seasoning.

4. Use a pizza wheel to cut each tortilla into 12 triangles.

5. Place a sausage on the wide end of a tortilla triangle and roll it toward the point. Place it on the prepared pan. Repeat until all of the sausages are wrapped.

6. Use a pastry brush to brush the pigs in a blanket with the melted butter, then sprinkle with a little more everything bagel seasoning.

7. Bake for 12 to 15 minutes, until the edges start to turn golden brown. Serve with cocktail toothpicks. Best served fresh.

NET CARBS 1.6g

calories	fat	protein	carbs	fiber
108	9.4g	3.7g	4.1g	2.5g

Jalapeño Corn Dog Poppers

yield 12 poppers (1 per serving) • *prep time* 15 minutes • *cook time* 20 minutes

1½ cups finely ground blanched almond flour

2 teaspoons baking powder

¼ teaspoon salt

2 large eggs

¼ cup unsweetened almond milk

2 tablespoons avocado oil, plus more for the pan

1 teaspoon sweet corn extract

½ cup shredded cheddar cheese

1 jalapeño pepper, seeded and finely chopped (optional)

3 beef hot dogs

1. Preheat the oven to 350°F. Grease a standard-size 12-well muffin pan with avocado oil.

2. In a small mixing bowl, whisk together the almond flour, baking powder, and salt.

3. In a medium-size mixing bowl, whisk the eggs, almond milk, oil, and corn extract. Slowly add the flour mixture while stirring with a rubber spatula until well blended. Fold in the cheese and jalapeño, if using, until well combined. Pour the batter into the prepared muffin pan, filling the wells about three-quarters full.

4. Cut each hot dog into 4 even pieces. Place a hot dog piece in the center of the batter in each well.

5. Bake for 15 to 20 minutes, until the tops are lightly browned. Allow to cool completely before removing from the pan.

Note

The jalapeño gives these poppers a nice kick, but you can leave it out for those who don't like it, or to make the poppers more kid-friendly.

	NET CARBS 1.6g			
calories	fat	protein	carbs	fiber
175	15.6g	6.4g	3.2g	1.5g

Personal Charcuterie Boards

yield 6 servings • *prep time* 10 minutes

24 slices hard salami

30 cubes cheddar cheese, white and/or yellow

60 almonds

18 blackberries

18 low-carb crackers, store-bought or homemade (page 122)

6 fresh rosemary sprigs

Special equipment: 6 small wood charcuterie boards

Arrange the ingredients on the boards, using the photo as a guide.

Notes

If the idea of planning and arranging your own large charcuterie board is a bit intimidating, this recipe takes away the guesswork. These individual-sized boards are perfectly portioned and ideal for those who prefer not to share from a communal serving platter.

Small boards like these can be found in many hobby and craft stores. Amazon.com and restaurant supply websites sell them as well. You also can use small cups, jars, paper cones, or paper boxes—be creative!

NET CARBS 3.8g

calories	fat	protein	carbs	fiber
319	25.9g	14.8g	7.2g	3.5g

Veggie Pizza

yield one 10 by 14-inch oval pizza (16 servings) • *prep time* 15 minutes (not including time to make dough) • *cook time* 18 minutes

1 recipe Multi-Purpose Dough (page 306)

1 (8-ounce) package cream cheese, softened

¼ cup mayonnaise

2 teaspoons dried dill weed

1 teaspoon dried parsley

1 teaspoon garlic powder

½ teaspoon onion powder

½ teaspoon salt

½ teaspoon ground black pepper

1 cup chopped broccoli

1 cup chopped cauliflower

¼ cup finely diced red bell pepper

1 cup shredded cheddar cheese

1. Preheat the oven to 375°F.

2. To make the crust, place the dough between two sheets of parchment paper. Use a rolling pin to roll the dough into an oval ¼ inch thick. Remove the top sheet of the parchment and slide the bottom sheet of parchment with the crust onto a pizza pan or baking sheet. Use a fork to lightly prick holes throughout the crust. Bake for 10 minutes, then remove from the oven and use a fork to pop any bubbles that have formed. Return the crust to the oven and bake until golden brown, 5 to 8 more minutes. Allow to cool.

3. In a medium-size mixing bowl, stir together the cream cheese, mayonnaise, dill, parsley, garlic powder, onion powder, salt, and pepper until well combined.

4. Spread the cream cheese mixture evenly over the top of the baked crust. Top the pizza with the broccoli, cauliflower, bell pepper, and cheese. Cut into 16 squares and serve.

Note ———

This cold appetizer pizza with its crunchy raw toppings was served at a lot of showers and similar functions when I was growing up. It is always a big hit!

Make Ahead ———

The dough can be made up to 2 days ahead. Store in an airtight container in the refrigerator.

NET CARBS 2.4g

calories	fat	protein	carbs	fiber
202	20.7g	7.9g	3.3g	0.9g

Kettle Corn

yield 8 cups (1 cup per serving) • *prep time* 2 minutes • *cook time* 3 minutes

¼ cup coconut oil

½ cup popcorn kernels

½ cup granular allulose

Flaky sea salt

Make Ahead

Can be made up to 1 day ahead. Store in an airtight container on the counter.

1. Line a sheet pan with parchment paper.

2. Heat the oil in a heavy-bottomed stainless-steel pot over medium-high heat. Add 3 popcorn kernels to the pot and cover with a lid.

3. When the kernels pop, add the rest of the kernels to the pot. Sprinkle with the allulose and use a wooden spoon to stir quickly until all of the kernels are coated. Put the lid back on the pot. Shake the pot continuously to make sure the bottom of the popcorn doesn't burn, listening for the kernels to pop as you shake. When the popping slows to 1 second between pops, remove the pot from the heat.

4. Carefully spread the hot popcorn evenly on the prepared pan. Sprinkle with flaky sea salt and allow to cool for 5 minutes before serving.

Notes

Popcorn isn't typical on a low-carb menu, but some people enjoy it in moderation, as it only has 5 grams of net carbs per serving.

For a fun movie night menu, pair this kettle corn with mugs of Hot Cocoa for a Crowd (page 84).

NET CARBS 5g				
calories	fat	protein	carbs	fiber
91	7.1g	1g	6.2g	1.2g

Slow Cooker Party Meatballs

yield 40 meatballs (20 servings as an appetizer, 10 servings as a meal) •
prep time 15 minutes • *cook time* 4 hours 20 minutes

2 pounds ground beef

2 large eggs

1 teaspoon salt

1 teaspoon ground black pepper

½ teaspoon garlic powder

½ teaspoon ground dried oregano

½ cup grated Parmesan cheese

½ cup finely crushed pork rinds

1 (12-ounce) jar grape jelly (no sugar added)

1½ cups barbecue sauce (no sugar added), store-bought or homemade (see page 305)

Chopped fresh parsley, for garnish (optional)

Special equipment (optional):
Cocktail toothpicks, for serving

Make Ahead

The meatball mixture can be made up to 2 days ahead, following Steps 2 and 3. Store in an airtight container in the refrigerator. The day of the gathering, follow Steps 1, 4, 5, and 6 to complete the recipe.

1. Preheat the oven to 400°F. Line a sheet pan with parchment paper.

2. Place the ground beef in a large mixing bowl and use your hands to gently break it up.

3. In a small mixing bowl, whisk together the eggs, salt, pepper, garlic powder, and oregano. Pour the egg mixture over the meat and sprinkle with the Parmesan cheese and pork rinds. Use your hands to gently mix the ingredients just until well combined; be careful not to overwork the meat.

4. Lightly roll the meat mixture into balls about 1¼ inches in diameter and place on the prepared pan, spaced about 1 inch apart. Bake the meatballs until lightly browned, 18 to 20 minutes.

5. Transfer the meatballs to a 6-quart slow cooker. Spoon the jelly and barbecue sauce evenly over the meatballs. Cook on low for 3 to 4 hours, until the meatballs are cooked through.

6. Lower the temperature to warm and allow guests to serve themselves directly from the slow cooker. Alternatively, transfer the meatballs to a serving dish and serve with cocktail toothpicks. Garnish with parsley, if desired.

NET CARBS 3.3g

calories	fat	protein	carbs	fiber
96	5.6g	6.4g	6.4g	3.1g

Baked Ham & Cheese Sliders

yield 9 sliders (1 per serving) • *prep time* 15 minutes (not including time to make rolls) • *cook time* 20 minutes

1 recipe Hawaiian Pull-Apart Rolls (page 238)

9 thin slices deli ham (about 8 ounces)

9 slices Swiss cheese (about 8 ounces)

2 tablespoons mayonnaise

¼ cup (½ stick) salted butter, melted

1 teaspoon dried minced onions

2 teaspoons Dijon mustard, plus more for serving if desired

1 teaspoon Worcestershire sauce

1 tablespoon poppy seeds

1. Preheat the oven to 350°F. Lightly spray an 11 by 7-inch baking dish with oil.

2. Slice the rolls in half horizontally. Place the bottom halves close together in the prepared baking dish. Top each with a slice of ham and a slice of cheese. Spread the cut side of the roll tops with the mayonnaise, then place them on top of the ham and cheese.

3. In a medium-size mixing bowl, whisk together the butter, dried minced onions, mustard, Worcestershire sauce, and poppy seeds. Drizzle the butter mixture over the tops of the sandwiches.

4. Cover with foil and bake for 15 minutes, until the cheese has melted. Remove the foil and bake for 3 to 5 more minutes, until the tops of the sandwiches are lightly browned. Let cool slightly, then use a knife to cut into individual sliders. Serve with additional mustard, if desired.

NET CARBS 2.3g

calories	fat	protein	carbs	fiber
375	30.9g	23.9g	3.5g	1.2g

Dill Pickle Dip

yield 8 servings • *prep time* 10 minutes, plus 2 hours to chill

1 cup sour cream

4 ounces cream cheese
(½ cup), softened

¼ cup mayonnaise

1 cup dill pickle slices, finely
chopped

2 tablespoons dill pickle juice

1 tablespoon Worcestershire
sauce

2 tablespoons chopped fresh
dill

2 teaspoons dried dill weed

1 teaspoon dried parsley

½ teaspoon garlic powder

½ teaspoon onion powder

½ teaspoon ground black
pepper

¼ teaspoon salt

In a large mixing bowl, stir together all of the ingredients until thoroughly combined. Refrigerate for least 2 hours before serving with the scoopers of your choice.

Serving suggestions:
Cooked bacon, cucumber
rounds, Parmesan crisps,
and/or pork rinds

Make Ahead —————
Can be made up to 3 days ahead. Store in an airtight container in the refrigerator.

NET CARBS 2.6g

calories	fat	protein	carbs	fiber
168	16.1g	2.1g	2.7g	0.1g

Creamy Dill Pickle Chopped Salad

yield 8 servings • *prep time* 15 minutes

Salad:

4 cups chopped romaine lettuce

1 cup finely chopped red cabbage

1 cup chopped cauliflower

¾ cup cubed white cheddar cheese

6 slices bacon, cooked and crumbled

½ cup chopped raw pecans

Dressing:

1 cup sour cream

½ cup mayonnaise

½ cup chopped dill pickles

¼ cup dill pickle juice

1 tablespoon chopped fresh dill

1 tablespoon chopped fresh parsley

2 teaspoons dried chives

1 teaspoon garlic powder

1 teaspoon onion powder

½ teaspoon salt

½ teaspoon ground black pepper

1. Place the lettuce in a serving bowl. Arrange the rest of the salad ingredients on top of the lettuce.

2. To make the dressing, put all of the dressing ingredients in a small mixing bowl and whisk until well combined.

3. Drizzle the dressing over the salad, toss well, and serve immediately.

Note

You don't have to carefully arrange the salad ingredients on top of the lettuce as shown. For a more informal presentation, simply put the rest of the salad ingredients on top of the lettuce, in no particular arrangement, then pour on the dressing and gently toss until the salad is coated with the dressing.

Make Ahead

The dressing can be made up to 3 days ahead. The salad ingredients (without the dressing) can be assembled up to a few hours before serving, but once dressed, the salad should be served immediately.

NET CARBS 3.4g

calories	fat	protein	carbs	fiber
344	32.1g	10.4g	5.2g	1.8g

BLT Chicken Salad

yield 6 servings • *prep time* 10 minutes, plus 1 hour to chill

3 cups shredded rotisserie chicken

1 celery rib, finely chopped

2 green onions, sliced

1 tablespoon chopped fresh parsley

½ cup mayonnaise

6 slices bacon, cooked and crumbled

1 cup grape or cherry tomatoes, halved

¼ teaspoon salt

¼ teaspoon ground black pepper

Lettuce leaves, for serving (optional)

1. Place the chicken, celery, green onions, parsley, mayonnaise, bacon, tomatoes, salt, and pepper in a medium-size mixing bowl and mix well. Taste and season with additional salt and pepper, if desired.

2. Refrigerate for at least 1 hour before serving. Serve on lettuce leaves, if desired.

Note ——————————

You can use your own cooked and shredded chicken breast or thigh meat instead of store-bought rotisserie chicken. However, your salad will not have as much flavor as a salad made with rotisserie chicken.

Make Ahead ——————

Can be made up to 3 days ahead. Store in an airtight container in the refrigerator.

NET CARBS 1.1g

calories	fat	protein	carbs	fiber
382	34.6g	18.9g	1.7g	0.6g

Zucchini Caprese Salad

yield 6 servings • *prep time* 15 minutes, plus 2 hours to chill

1 large zucchini

4 ounces marinated fresh mini mozzarella balls, halved

4 ounces grape or cherry tomatoes, halved

Dressing:

2 tablespoons extra-virgin olive oil

2 teaspoons balsamic vinegar

Juice of 1 lemon

8 fresh basil leaves, chopped

1 clove garlic, minced

½ teaspoon ground dried oregano

½ teaspoon ground black pepper

¼ teaspoon salt

1. Quarter the zucchini lengthwise, then slice it crosswise into quarter-moons. Place the zucchini in a medium-size serving bowl along with the mozzarella balls and tomatoes.

2. To make the dressing, put all of the dressing ingredients in a small mixing bowl and whisk until well combined.

3. Pour the dressing over the zucchini mixture and gently toss until the salad ingredients are well combined and evenly coated in the dressing. Refrigerate for at least 2 hours before serving.

Note ————

If you prefer, you may spiral-slice the zucchini.

Make Ahead ————

Can be made up to 1 day ahead. Store in an airtight container in the refrigerator.

NET CARBS 3.2g

calories	fat	protein	carbs	fiber
112	8.8g	5g	4.2g	1g

Buffalo Cobb Salad

yield 6 servings • *prep time* 15 minutes (not including time to make Buffalo sauce or dressing) • *cook time* 20 minutes

Buffalo chicken:

1½ pounds chicken breast tenderloins

2 tablespoons avocado oil

1 teaspoon paprika

½ teaspoon chili powder

½ teaspoon garlic powder

½ teaspoon salt

½ teaspoon ground black pepper

¼ cup Buffalo Sauce (page 304)

4 cups chopped romaine lettuce

8 slices bacon, cooked and crumbled

4 ounces grape or cherry tomatoes, halved

4 hard-boiled eggs, sliced in half

1 medium cucumber, quartered lengthwise, then sliced crosswise

½ medium red onion, finely diced

½ cup crumbled blue cheese

1 cup Blue Cheese Dressing (page 303)

1. Preheat the oven to 375°F. Line a sheet pan with parchment paper.

2. Place the chicken in a large resealable plastic bag, then pour the oil into the bag. Move the tenderloins around, ensuring all of the pieces get coated in the oil.

3. In a small mixing bowl, whisk together the paprika, chili powder, garlic powder, salt, and pepper. Pour into the bag with the chicken. Seal the bag and shake to coat the chicken in the seasonings.

4. Transfer the chicken to the prepared pan and bake for 20 minutes, or until the internal temperature reaches 165°F. Toss the tenderloins in the Buffalo sauce and set aside.

5. Place the lettuce in a large serving bowl. Arrange the chicken and the rest of the salad ingredients on top of the lettuce. Serve with the dressing alongside.

Note

You can serve this salad with cheddar cheese instead of blue cheese and Ranch Dressing (page 302) instead of blue cheese dressing.

Make Ahead

The chicken and dressing can be made up to 2 days ahead. Store in separate airtight containers in the refrigerator. Assemble the salad (without the dressing) up to a few hours before serving.

NET CARBS 4.8g

calories	fat	protein	carbs	fiber
662	53.9g	40g	6.3g	1.6g

Blueberry & Feta Arugula Salad

yield 6 servings • *prep time* 10 minutes

Salad:

6 cups arugula

¾ cup blueberries

½ cup sliced red onions

¼ cup sliced almonds

½ cup crumbled feta cheese

Dressing:

⅓ cup extra-virgin olive oil

2 tablespoons balsamic vinegar

1 teaspoon Dijon mustard

½ teaspoon granular sweetener

¼ teaspoon salt

¼ teaspoon ground black pepper

1. Place the arugula in a large serving bowl. Top with the blueberries, onions, almonds, and feta.

2. To make the dressing, put all of the dressing ingredients in a small mixing bowl and whisk until well combined.

3. Toss the salad and serve with the dressing alongside.

Note

To make this salad a meal, you can add your choice of protein. Steak, shrimp, and chicken are great options.

	NET CARBS 4.4g			
calories	fat	protein	carbs	fiber
190	17.4g	3.4g	5.9g	1.5g

Hearty Spaghetti Salad

yield 8 servings • *prep time* 20 minutes, plus 2 hours to chill • *cook time* 8 minutes

Salad:

1 (12-ounce) package hearts of palm angel hair pasta

1 medium cucumber, quartered lengthwise, then sliced crosswise

8 ounces grape or cherry tomatoes, halved

½ medium red bell pepper, chopped

½ small red onion, chopped

4 ounces marinated fresh mini mozzarella balls, halved

1 (4-ounce) can sliced black olives

8 ounces mini pepperoni slices

Dressing:

½ cup extra-virgin olive oil

¼ cup red wine vinegar

2 tablespoons grated Parmesan cheese

1 clove garlic, minced

1 teaspoon granular sweetener

½ teaspoon ground dried oregano

½ teaspoon dried basil

½ teaspoon dried parsley

½ teaspoon ground black pepper

¼ teaspoon salt

1. Bring a large pot of water to a boil. Place the hearts of palm pasta in the boiling water. Boil for 8 minutes. Pour the pasta into a colander to thoroughly drain. Use paper towels to pat off any excess water.

2. Transfer the pasta to a large serving bowl. Put the rest of the salad ingredients on top.

3. To make the dressing, put all of the dressing ingredients in a small mixing bowl and whisk until well combined.

4. Drizzle the dressing over the salad. Gently toss until all of the salad ingredients are coated with the dressing. Cover and refrigerate for at least 2 hours. Toss the salad again before serving.

Make Ahead

Can be made up to 2 days ahead. Store in an airtight container in the refrigerator.

	NET CARBS 3.5g			
calories	fat	protein	carbs	fiber
340	30.5g	10.5g	5.5g	2g

Shrimp Salad

yield 4 servings • *prep time* 10 minutes, plus 2 hours to chill • *cook time* 8 minutes

1 pound medium shrimp, peeled and deveined

1 tablespoon avocado oil

Salt and pepper

½ cup mayonnaise

¼ cup chopped celery

2 tablespoons finely chopped red onions

1 tablespoon freshly squeezed lime juice

1 teaspoon chopped fresh dill, plus more for garnish if desired

½ teaspoon Old Bay seasoning

1. Preheat the oven to 400°F. Line a sheet pan with parchment paper.

2. Pat the shrimp dry. Place the shrimp in a medium-size mixing bowl and drizzle with the oil. Gently toss until all of the shrimp are coated. Arrange the shrimp in a single layer on the prepared pan. Season with a pinch each of salt and pepper.

3. Roast for 6 to 8 minutes, until the shrimp are pink and opaque.

4. In a large serving bowl, mix together the mayonnaise, celery, onions, lime juice, dill, and Old Bay seasoning. Add the cooked shrimp and toss until evenly coated in the dressing. Garnish with extra dill, if desired. Refrigerate for at least 2 hours before serving.

Make Ahead

Can be made up to 2 days ahead. Store in an airtight container in the refrigerator.

NET CARBS 1.3g

calories	fat	protein	carbs	fiber
311	28.4g	16.5g	1.5g	0.2g

Greek Salad

yield 6 servings • *prep time* 15 minutes

Salad:

1 medium English cucumber, quartered lengthwise and then sliced crosswise

4 ounces cherry tomatoes, halved

1 medium orange bell pepper, chopped

½ small red onion, finely chopped

2 teaspoons chopped fresh oregano, or ¾ teaspoon dried oregano leaves

1 cup Kalamata olives, pitted

½ cup crumbled feta cheese

Dressing:

¼ cup extra-virgin olive oil

2 tablespoons red wine vinegar

1 tablespoon freshly squeezed lemon juice

1 teaspoon ground dried oregano

½ teaspoon salt

¼ teaspoon ground black pepper

1. Place the cucumber, tomatoes, bell pepper, onion, oregano, and olives in a medium-size serving bowl. Gently toss the salad ingredients together.

2. To make the dressing, put all of the dressing ingredients in a small mixing bowl and whisk until well combined.

3. Drizzle the dressing over the salad and toss until the salad ingredients are well coated. Add the feta and gently toss once more. Serve immediately.

Note

Best served immediately but can be assembled (without the dressing) up to a few hours before serving.

NET CARBS 3.7g

calories	fat	protein	carbs	fiber
207	18.8g	4.5g	5.4g	1.7g

Egg Roll Soup

yield 6 servings • *prep time* 10 minutes • *cook time* 26 minutes

1 pound bulk breakfast sausage

½ cup finely diced onions

1 carrot, diced

3 cloves garlic, minced

1 small head green cabbage, roughly shredded

4 cups vegetable broth

¼ cup coconut aminos

2 teaspoons ginger powder

1 teaspoon ground black pepper

Salt

2 teaspoons toasted sesame oil

Suggested garnishes:

Toasted sesame seeds

Sliced green onions

1. Put the sausage, onions, and carrot in a stockpot over medium heat. Cook, crumbling the sausage, until the meat is browned and the vegetables are tender, about 10 minutes. Add the garlic and cook for 1 more minute. Drain if necessary.

2. Stir in the cabbage, broth, aminos, ginger, and pepper. Continue cooking the soup for 15 minutes, until the cabbage is tender.

3. Stir in the oil. Season to taste with salt and additional pepper. Garnish with sesame seeds and sliced green onions, if desired, and serve.

Make Ahead

Can be made up to 2 days ahead. Store in an airtight container in the refrigerator. Reheat in a stockpot over medium-low heat. Garnish the soup just before serving.

NET CARBS 5.6g

calories	fat	protein	carbs	fiber
298	24.3g	11.7g	8.1g	2.4g

Slow Cooker Chili for a Crowd

yield 12 servings • *prep time* 15 minutes • *cook time* 4½ to 6½ hours

4 pounds ground beef

10 slices bacon, diced

1 medium onion, diced

4 cloves garlic, minced

1 (28-ounce) can tomato sauce

1 (28-ounce) can petite diced tomatoes

2 cups vegetable broth

5 tablespoons chili powder

3 tablespoons ground cumin

2 teaspoons ground dried oregano

2 teaspoons paprika

1 teaspoon cocoa powder

1 teaspoon salt

1 teaspoon ground black pepper

Serving suggestions:

Sour cream, sliced green onions or diced red onions, shredded cheddar cheese, and/or low-carb tortilla chips

1. Cook the ground beef, bacon, onion, and garlic in batches in a large skillet over medium heat, crumbling the meat as it cooks, until the meat is browned, about 10 minutes per batch. Drain if necessary.

2. Put the meat mixture in a 6-quart slow cooker. Pour in the tomato sauce, diced tomatoes, and broth. Stir in the rest of the ingredients. Place the lid on the slow cooker and cook on low for 4 to 6 hours. The longer it cooks, the more flavor it will develop.

Note

Chili with fixings is an easy buffet meal for entertaining. Serve with the suggested toppings or with any fixings of your choice. I purposely made this chili minimally spicy to appeal to everyone. Sliced fresh or pickled jalapeños and/or various hot sauces are good additions to a chili buffet to allow guests to customize the heat level of their bowl.

Make Ahead

Can be made up to 3 days ahead. Store in an airtight container in the refrigerator. To reheat, turn the slow cooker to warm. Alternatively, you can complete Step 1 up to 2 days in advance and finish the recipe the day of the gathering.

NET CARBS 6g

calories	fat	protein	carbs	fiber
282	19.2g	16.9g	8.9g	2.9g

Creamy Tuscan Chicken Soup

yield 6 servings • *prep time* 15 minutes • *cook time* 35 minutes

2 tablespoons salted butter

1 pound boneless, skinless chicken thighs, cut into bite-size pieces

Salt and pepper

4 slices bacon, diced

½ cup diced onions

2 cloves garlic, minced

3 cups chicken broth

1 (14½-ounce) can petite diced tomatoes

2 tablespoons chopped fresh parsley

1 tablespoon chopped fresh basil

1 teaspoon ground dried oregano

½ teaspoon paprika

2 cups baby spinach

½ cup heavy whipping cream

Grated Parmesan cheese, for serving (optional)

1. Melt the butter in a stockpot over medium-high heat. Lightly season the chicken with salt and pepper. Cook the chicken and bacon until the chicken is browned on both sides and the bacon is cooked through, about 10 minutes.

2. Add the onions and garlic and cook until the onions are tender, about 5 minutes. Pour in the broth and tomatoes, then stir in the parsley, basil, oregano, and paprika. Bring to a boil, then lower the heat and simmer for 10 minutes, stirring occasionally.

3. Stir in the spinach and cream and cook until the spinach is wilted and the cream is heated through, about 10 more minutes. Season with salt and pepper to taste. Serve with grated Parmesan cheese, if desired.

Make Ahead

Can be made up to 2 days ahead. Store in an airtight container in the refrigerator. Reheat in a stockpot over low heat.

	NET CARBS 2.9g			
calories	fat	protein	carbs	fiber
265	17.3g	23.2g	4.5g	1.6g

Lasagna Soup

yield 8 servings • *prep time* 15 minutes • *cook time* 35 minutes

8 ounces ground beef

8 ounces bulk breakfast sausage

¼ cup diced onions

2 cloves garlic, minced

1 cup low-sugar marinara sauce

1 (14½-ounce) can petite diced tomatoes

2½ cups vegetable broth

1 medium zucchini, diced

2 teaspoons dried basil

2 teaspoons ground dried oregano

2 teaspoons dried parsley

½ teaspoon salt

½ teaspoon ground black pepper

Topping:

10 ounces ricotta cheese

1 cup shredded mozzarella cheese

½ cup grated Parmesan cheese

Fresh parsley, for garnish (optional)

1. Cook the ground beef, sausage, onions, and garlic in a stockpot over medium heat, crumbling the meat as it cooks, until the meat is browned, about 10 minutes. Drain if necessary.

2. Stir in the marinara sauce, tomatoes, broth, zucchini, and seasonings. Bring to a low boil and cook until the zucchini is tender, about 5 minutes. Reduce the heat to low and simmer for 20 more minutes to allow the flavors to develop.

3. While the soup simmers, make the topping: In a small mixing bowl, stir together the ricotta, mozzarella, and Parmesan.

4. Dollop spoonfuls of the cheese mixture on top of the soup before serving, either on the soup directly in the pot or on individual servings. Garnish with parsley, if desired.

Make Ahead

You can make the soup and topping, completing Steps 1 through 3, up to 3 days ahead. Store in separate airtight containers in the refrigerator. Reheat the soup in a stockpot over low heat, then garnish with the topping.

	NET CARBS 6.1g			
calories	fat	protein	carbs	fiber
343	24.7g	21.2g	8.1g	2g

Sausage Corn Chowder

yield 6 servings • *prep time* 10 minutes • *cook time* 30 minutes

1 pound bulk breakfast sausage

½ cup diced red bell peppers

2 green onions, sliced, plus more for garnish if desired

1 (15-ounce) can baby corn, drained and cut into bite-size pieces

1½ cups heavy whipping cream

1½ cups vegetable broth

½ teaspoon ground black pepper

½ teaspoon xanthan gum

¼ teaspoon sweet corn extract (optional)

Salt

1. Cook the sausage, bell peppers, and green onions in a stockpot over medium heat, crumbling the meat as it cooks, until the meat is browned, about 10 minutes. Drain if necessary.

2. Add the corn, cream, and broth. Stir in the black pepper and xanthan gum. Continue cooking, stirring frequently, until the chowder starts to thicken, about 10 minutes.

3. Stir in the corn extract, if using, and turn the heat to low. Let simmer for 10 more minutes, then season with salt to taste. Serve garnished with sliced green onions, if desired.

Make Ahead

The soup can be made up to 2 days ahead. Reheat in a stockpot over low heat. Garnish with the green onions, if using, just before serving.

NET CARBS 1.9g

calories	fat	protein	carbs	fiber
446	43g	11.7g	4g	2.1g

Blender Gazpacho

yield 8 servings • *prep time* 10 minutes, plus 4 hours to chill

6 Roma tomatoes

1 small cucumber, peeled

1 medium green bell pepper

½ medium onion

2 cloves garlic, chopped

2 tablespoons chopped fresh parsley, plus more for garnish if desired

1 cup vegetable juice

2 tablespoons red wine vinegar

2 tablespoons extra-virgin olive oil

2 teaspoons Worcestershire sauce

1 teaspoon salt

1 teaspoon ground black pepper

½ teaspoon smoked paprika

Sour cream, for garnish (optional)

1. Cut the tomatoes, cucumber, bell pepper, and onion into large chunks and place in a blender.

2. Add the rest of the ingredients and blend until the desired consistency is achieved. Some people like gazpacho smooth; I prefer it slightly chunky.

3. Pour the soup into an airtight container. Refrigerate for at least 4 hours or ideally overnight to allow the flavors to develop.

4. Serve garnished with sour cream and parsley, if desired.

Make Ahead

Can be made up to 2 days ahead. Store in an airtight container in the refrigerator.

	NET CARBS 3.9g			
calories	fat	protein	carbs	fiber
57	3.7g	1.2g	5.4g	1.5g

CHAPTER 5

Mains

Crab & Shrimp Étouffée

yield 8 servings • *prep time* 20 minutes • *cook time* 40 minutes

2 tablespoons salted butter

2 tablespoons finely ground blanched almond flour

1 tablespoon coconut flour

2 cloves garlic, minced

1 medium onion, chopped

1 medium green bell pepper, chopped

2 celery ribs, diced

4 cups vegetable or seafood broth

1 (14½-ounce) can petite diced tomatoes

2 tablespoons chopped fresh parsley, plus more for garnish if desired

1 teaspoon Worcestershire sauce

1 teaspoon ground black pepper

½ teaspoon cayenne pepper

½ teaspoon ground dried oregano

½ teaspoon paprika

½ teaspoon salt

¼ teaspoon onion powder

2 bay leaves

1 pound medium shrimp, peeled and deveined

8 ounces lump crab meat

4 cups cooked cauliflower rice, for serving

1. To make the roux, melt the butter in a stockpot over medium heat. Add the almond flour and coconut flour and cook, stirring constantly, until the roux turns dark brown, about 10 minutes.

2. Add the garlic, onion, bell pepper, and celery to the pot and cook, stirring occasionally, until the vegetables are tender, about 10 minutes.

3. Pour the broth and tomatoes into the pot and stir to combine. Stir in the parsley, Worcestershire sauce, black pepper, cayenne pepper, oregano, paprika, salt, onion powder, and bay leaves. Bring to a boil and cook for 15 minutes, stirring occasionally.

4. Stir in the shrimp and crab meat and simmer until the shrimp turn pink and are cooked through, about 5 minutes. Reduce the heat to low to keep the stew warm until ready to serve; once the shrimp are cooked, avoid simmering the étouffée, or the shrimp will become overcooked. Serve with the cauliflower rice and garnish with parsley, if desired.

Make Ahead

Complete Steps 1 through 3 up to 2 days ahead. Store in an airtight container in the refrigerator. When reheating, add the shrimp and crab and simmer until cooked, following Step 4. Then serve as directed.

NET CARBS 5.3g

calories	fat	protein	carbs	fiber
128	3.8g	14.6g	8.2g	2.9g

Pecan-Crusted Salmon

yield 4 servings • *prep time* 10 minutes • *cook time* 18 minutes

1 (1-pound) salmon fillet

½ teaspoon salt

½ teaspoon ground black pepper

1 tablespoon Dijon mustard

1 tablespoon sugar-free maple syrup

⅓ cup finely chopped raw pecans

Chopped fresh parsley, for garnish (optional)

4 lemon wedges, for serving

1. Preheat the oven to 400°F. Line a sheet pan with parchment paper.

2. Place the salmon skin side down on the prepared pan. Pat it dry with paper towels. Season with the salt and pepper.

3. In a small mixing bowl, mix the mustard and maple syrup, then brush the top of the salmon with the mixture. Gently press the pecans on the salmon.

4. Bake the salmon for 15 to 18 minutes, depending on thickness, until it is cooked through. It should easily flake with a fork when done and have a temperature of 135°F in the thickest part. Garnish with parsley, if desired, and serve with lemon wedges. Best eaten the same day.

NET CARBS 0.7g

calories	fat	protein	carbs	fiber
242	13.7g	25.6g	5.4g	4.7g

Asian-Inspired Beef Cups

yield 4 servings as a meal, 8 servings as an appetizer • *prep time* 10 minutes • *cook time* 22 minutes

2 teaspoons toasted sesame oil, divided

1 pound ground beef

½ cup diced red bell peppers

3 cloves garlic, minced

2 tablespoons coconut aminos

2 teaspoons unseasoned rice vinegar

2 tablespoons brown sugar substitute

2 teaspoons ginger powder

8 medium butter lettuce leaves, for serving

For garnish:

2 green onions, sliced

1 teaspoon toasted sesame seeds

¼ cup unsalted roasted peanuts, chopped

1. Heat 1 teaspoon of the oil in a large skillet over medium heat. Cook the ground beef and bell peppers in the skillet, crumbling the beef as it cooks, until the meat is browned and the peppers are tender, about 10 minutes. Add the garlic and cook for 1 more minute. Drain if necessary.

2. Stir in the aminos, vinegar, brown sugar substitute, ginger powder, and remaining 1 teaspoon of oil. Continue cooking, stirring frequently, until the mixture thickens, about 10 minutes.

3. Serve in the lettuce leaves. Garnish with the green onions, toasted sesame seeds, and peanuts.

Note

These beef cups are an additive- and sweetener-free twist on a popular dish from a large restaurant chain. They can be served as a main dish or an appetizer. The cups also make a great self-serve buffet "bar" option: simply set out the lettuce leaves, cooked meat filling, and garnishes and allow guests to construct their own. The Cilantro Lime Coleslaw on page 240 would be a nice addition to an Asian-Inspired Beef Cups bar.

Make Ahead

The meat can be made up to 1 day ahead and reheated before serving. Store in an airtight container in the refrigerator.

NET CARBS 2.1g

calories	fat	protein	carbs	fiber
203	15.9g	11.7g	3.3g	1.2g

Cajun Shrimp Alfredo

yield 6 servings • *prep time* 10 minutes • *cook time* 22 minutes

4 tablespoons (½ stick) salted butter, divided

1 pound medium shrimp, peeled and deveined

1 tablespoon Cajun seasoning

¼ teaspoon cayenne pepper

4 cloves garlic, minced

1 cup grated Parmesan cheese

½ cup heavy whipping cream

1 (12-ounce) package hearts of palm angel hair pasta

Sliced green onions, for garnish (optional)

1. Melt 2 tablespoons of the butter in a large deep skillet over medium heat. Place the shrimp in the skillet and sprinkle with the Cajun seasoning and cayenne pepper. Cook until the shrimp turn pink, 4 to 5 minutes. Remove the shrimp from the skillet.

2. In the same skillet, still over medium heat, melt the remaining 2 tablespoons of butter. Cook the garlic until fragrant, 1 to 2 minutes. Stir in the Parmesan and cream and cook, stirring often, until creamy and well combined, about 5 minutes.

3. Stir the pasta into the sauce and cook for 10 more minutes, or until the noodles are softened. Divide the pasta among six plates or shallow serving bowls and top evenly with the cooked shrimp. Garnish with green onions, if desired, and serve.

NET CARBS 2.2g

calories	fat	protein	carbs	fiber
236	17.8g	19g	3.9g	1.6g

Roasted Rosemary Chicken Thighs & Radishes

yield 6 servings • *prep time* 10 minutes • *cook time* 30 minutes

6 boneless, skinless chicken thighs (about 1½ pounds)

2 tablespoons avocado oil

1 tablespoon chopped fresh rosemary, plus fresh rosemary sprigs for garnish if desired

1 teaspoon ground dried oregano

½ teaspoon salt

¼ teaspoon ground black pepper

6 thin lemon slices

10 ounces radishes, trimmed and halved

2 tablespoons salted butter, melted

1. Preheat the oven to 425°F. Grease a sheet pan with avocado oil.

2. Arrange the chicken thighs on the prepared pan. In a small mixing bowl, whisk together the oil, rosemary, oregano, salt, and pepper. Brush both sides of the chicken with the oil mixture, making sure each piece is well coated. Place a lemon slice on each piece of chicken.

3. Toss the radishes with the melted butter and arrange them on the pan between the pieces of chicken. Bake for 30 minutes, or until the chicken reaches an internal temperature of 165°F and the radishes are tender. Serve garnished with rosemary sprigs, if desired.

NET CARBS 1.1g

calories	fat	protein	carbs	fiber
222	13.3g	22.7g	2.1g	1g

Parmesan Garlic Wings

yield 4 servings as a meal, 8 servings as an appetizer • *prep time* 10 minutes • *cook time* 37 minutes

2 pounds chicken wings

½ teaspoon salt

½ teaspoon ground black pepper

¼ teaspoon ground dried oregano

¼ teaspoon onion powder

¼ cup (½ stick) salted butter, melted

2 cloves garlic, minced

⅓ cup grated Parmesan cheese

2 tablespoons chopped fresh parsley, plus more for garnish if desired

1. Preheat the oven to 400°F. Line a sheet pan with parchment paper.

2. Pat the wings dry and arrange in a single layer on the prepared pan. In a small mixing bowl, whisk together the salt, pepper, oregano, and onion powder. Sprinkle the seasoning mixture evenly on the wings.

3. Bake for 30 to 35 minutes, until the wings are browned and cooked through. The internal temperature should be 165°F.

4. In a medium-size mixing bowl, stir together the melted butter, garlic, Parmesan, and parsley. Put the wings in the bowl and gently toss until they are coated in the sauce.

5. Turn the oven to the broil setting. Return the wings to the sheet pan and broil for 2 minutes to brown the tops. Serve immediately, garnished with parsley, if desired.

Notes

You can double the butter sauce if you'd like more for dipping. Simply pour off half after making it, following Step 4, before adding the wings to the bowl.

The nutrition information below is based on 8 servings.

NET CARBS 0.4g

calories	fat	protein	carbs	fiber
279	20.9g	21.1g	0.4g	0g

Cheesy Chicken & Rice

yield 6 servings • *prep time* 10 minutes • *cook time* 25 minutes

2 tablespoons salted butter

1½ pounds boneless, skinless chicken thighs

¼ cup chopped onions

1 clove garlic, minced

1 tablespoon ground cumin

2 teaspoons chili powder

1 teaspoon paprika

½ teaspoon ground dried oregano

½ teaspoon salt

½ teaspoon ground black pepper

1 (4-ounce) can diced green chilies

1½ cups shredded Monterey Jack cheese

2 tablespoons heavy whipping cream

2 cups cooked cauliflower rice

Chopped fresh cilantro, for garnish (optional)

1. Melt the butter in a large deep skillet over medium heat, then add the chicken, onions, and garlic and cook until the chicken is no longer pink in the center, about 10 minutes. Use two forks to shred the chicken in the skillet.

2. Stir in the cumin, chili powder, paprika, oregano, salt, pepper, and green chilies. Continue cooking for 10 more minutes.

3. Add the cheese and cream and mix until the cheese has melted, then stir in the cauliflower rice. Serve garnished with cilantro, if desired.

Note

My daughter loves the chicken, cheese, and rice dish called pollo loco at our local Mexican restaurant, and this is my spin on it. Try serving it with low-carb tortillas, topped with sour cream, guacamole, and/or salsa.

NET CARBS 2.4g

calories	fat	protein	carbs	fiber
410	26.7g	37g	4.1g	1.7g

Loaded Ranch Pork Chops

yield 6 servings • *prep time* 10 minutes, plus 30 minutes to marinate • *cook time* 30 minutes

Marinade:

2 tablespoons extra-virgin olive oil

½ teaspoon salt

½ teaspoon ground black pepper

½ teaspoon garlic powder

6 boneless pork loin chops (about 1¼ pounds)

1 (8-ounce) package cream cheese, softened

¼ cup mayonnaise

1 cup shredded cheddar cheese

¼ cup sliced green onions, plus more for garnish

2 teaspoons dried parsley

1 teaspoon dried dill weed

1 teaspoon dried minced onions

¼ teaspoon garlic powder

¼ teaspoon ground black pepper

6 slices bacon, cooked and crumbled, for garnish

1. In a small mixing bowl, whisk together the ingredients for the marinade. Place the pork chops in a large resealable plastic bag, then drizzle the marinade over the chops. Seal the bag and gently toss to coat the chops. Put the chops in the refrigerator to marinate for 30 minutes.

2. Preheat the oven to 350°F. Grease a 13 by 9-inch baking dish with oil.

3. In a small mixing bowl, mix together the cream cheese, mayonnaise, cheddar cheese, and green onions until well combined. Stir in the parsley, dill, dried minced onions, garlic powder, and pepper.

4. Place the pork chops in the prepared baking dish and evenly spoon the cheese mixture on top. Bake for 25 to 30 minutes, until the juices run clear and the internal temperature reaches 145°F. Let the chops rest for 10 minutes.

5. Garnish the pork chops with the bacon and green onions and serve.

Note

You can also make this recipe with the same quantity of chicken breast.

NET CARBS 1.4g

calories	fat	protein	carbs	fiber
532	45g	29.8g	1.7g	0.3g

Maple & Brown Sugar–Glazed Spiral Ham

yield 10 to 12 servings • *prep time* 10 minutes, plus 1 hour to temper and 20 minutes to rest • *cook time* 1¼ to 1¾ hours, depending on size of ham

1 (5- to 7-pound) bone-in, fully cooked spiral-sliced ham

Glaze:

½ cup (1 stick) salted butter

¼ cup brown sugar substitute

2 tablespoons sugar-free maple syrup

½ teaspoon ground cinnamon

¼ teaspoon garlic powder

2 teaspoons pure pineapple extract

Note

This ham makes an excellent addition to a grazing table. Serve with Hawaiian Pull-Apart Rolls (page 238), cutting the ham into pieces about the size of the rolls.

1. Remove the ham from the refrigerator and let rest at room temperature for 1 hour.

2. Preheat the oven to 275°F.

3. To make the glaze, melt the butter in a medium-size saucepan over low heat. Whisk in the brown sugar substitute, maple syrup, cinnamon, and garlic powder. Bring the mixture to a boil for 1 minute, whisking continuously. Remove the pan from the heat and stir in the pineapple extract.

4. Place the ham in a roasting pan. Brush the ham with half of the glaze. Cover with foil. Bake for 15 minutes per pound of ham. Halfway through baking, baste the ham with the juices in the bottom of the pan.

5. Remove the ham from the oven. Increase the temperature to 400°F. Brush the ham with the rest of the glaze and bake uncovered for 10 to 15 more minutes, until the internal temperature reaches 140°F. Let the ham rest for 20 minutes before serving.

Make Ahead

Can be made up to 2 days ahead and served reheated or cold. Store in an airtight container in the refrigerator.

NET CARBS 4.2g

calories	fat	protein	carbs	fiber
223	16.6g	14.1g	6.6g	2.4g

Sesame Chicken

yield 4 servings • *prep time* 20 minutes • *cook time* 20 minutes

2 large eggs

½ cup whey protein powder (unflavored and unsweetened)

½ teaspoon salt

½ teaspoon ground black pepper

1 pound boneless, skinless chicken thighs, cut into bite-size pieces

High-quality oil, for frying

Sauce:

¼ cup coconut aminos

¼ cup water

⅓ cup brown sugar substitute

¼ cup unseasoned rice vinegar

1 tablespoon toasted sesame oil

2 cloves garlic, minced

1 teaspoon ginger powder

1 tablespoon toasted sesame seeds, plus more for garnish

¼ teaspoon xanthan gum

2 cups cooked cauliflower rice, for serving

Sliced green onions, for garnish

1. Prepare the breading station: In a shallow dish, whisk the eggs. In another shallow dish, whisk together the whey protein, salt, and pepper.

2. Dip the chicken pieces in the egg a few at a time, allowing the excess egg to drip back into the bowl. Then dip the chicken in the whey protein mixture, making sure to coat all sides. Place the breaded pieces on a large plate. Repeat until all of the chicken pieces are breaded. (*Tip:* Use tongs because whey breading tends to be stickier than breading made with regular flour.)

3. Heat ½ inch of oil in a large deep skillet over medium heat. To test the temperature of the oil, dip the end of a wooden spoon handle into it; if bubbles form around the handle, it's ready. Working in a couple of batches to avoid crowding, fry the chicken for 3 to 4 minutes, then use tongs to gently turn the pieces and cook for 3 to 4 more minutes, until cooked through and golden brown on all sides. Put the chicken on a paper towel–lined plate to drain the grease, then transfer to a medium-size mixing bowl.

4. Prepare the sauce: In a medium-size saucepan over medium heat, whisk together the aminos, water, brown sugar substitute, vinegar, oil, garlic, ginger powder, and sesame seeds. Bring to a boil while continuing to whisk. Reduce the heat to low and sprinkle the xanthan gum on the sauce. Whisk until the sauce starts to thicken, then remove the pan from the heat.

5. Pour the sauce over the chicken and gently toss to coat, being careful not to dislodge any breading. Serve with cauliflower rice and garnish with sliced green onions and toasted sesame seeds.

NET CARBS 2.8g

calories	fat	protein	carbs	fiber
301	7.8g	51.1g	4.3g	1.4g

Walking Taco Bar

yield 12 tacos (1 per serving) • *prep time* 15 minutes (not including time to make seasoning and guacamole) • *cook time* 30 minutes

2 pounds ground beef

¼ cup water

¼ cup Taco Seasoning (page 300)

Toppings:

1 medium head iceberg lettuce, shredded

2 medium tomatoes, diced

2 cups shredded cheddar cheese

6 green onions, sliced

1 (4-ounce) can sliced black olives

1 (16-ounce) container sour cream

1 recipe Large Batch Guacamole (page 142)

12 (1.1-ounce) bags low-carb tortilla chips

1. In a large skillet over medium heat, brown the ground beef in a couple of batches, using a wooden spoon to crumble it, about 10 minutes per batch. Add the first batch of cooked beef to the pan with the second batch and stir in the water and taco seasoning. Cook for 10 more minutes, stirring occasionally. Remove from the heat and transfer the meat to a serving bowl.

2. Place the toppings in individual serving bowls. Serve the taco meat and toppings with the bagged tortilla chips. Allow guests the option to top their "tacos" with whatever they like.

Notes

This recipe got its name because the original version uses single-serving bags of corn chips as the serving vessel, making it an easy thing to eat on the go. I use Quest or Hilo tortilla chips instead; you can find both brands in grocery stores and on Amazon.com. Walking tacos make a great buffet spread, maybe paired with Slow Cooker Chili for a Crowd (page 196), or they could be a part of a larger Mexican-themed menu (see page 16).

The nutrition information below is for the meat and toppings only; chips brands vary.

Make Ahead

The taco meat can be made up to 1 day ahead. Store in an airtight container in the refrigerator. To reheat, place in a large skillet over low heat until warmed thoroughly.

NET CARBS 3.3g

calories	fat	protein	carbs	fiber
385	30.3g	19.3g	5g	1.7g

Bacon-Wrapped Stuffed Pork Tenderloin

yield 8 to 10 servings • *prep time* 25 minutes • *cook time* 1 hour

2 tablespoons salted butter

½ cup chopped onions

2 celery ribs, chopped

½ cup finely crushed pork rinds

1 large egg

2 teaspoons ground dried sage

¼ teaspoon salt

¼ teaspoon ground black pepper

1 (2- to 2½-pound) pork tenderloin

8 slices bacon

Freshly ground black pepper

Fresh parsley sprigs, for garnish (optional)

Make Ahead

Can be made up to 1 day ahead and baked the day of serving. Wrap the prepared tenderloin tightly in plastic wrap and store in an airtight container in the refrigerator. Allow to temper on the counter for 15 minutes before baking.

1. Preheat the oven to 450°F. Line a sheet pan with parchment paper.

2. Melt the butter in a medium-size skillet over medium heat. Add the onions and celery and cook until the vegetables are tender, about 10 minutes.

3. Transfer the cooked vegetables to a medium-size mixing bowl. Stir in the pork rinds, egg, sage, salt, and pepper until the ingredients are well combined.

4. Butterfly the tenderloin: Place the tenderloin on a cutting board. Cut a deep slit lengthwise down the side of the tenderloin about ½ inch from the bottom, being careful not to cut all the way through. Open the tenderloin like a book. Cover it with plastic wrap or parchment paper. Use a meat mallet to flatten the tenderloin to about a ½-inch thickness.

5. Spread the vegetable mixture evenly over the tenderloin, leaving a ½-inch border around the edges. Starting with the bottom long edge, roll the tenderloin in a spiral pattern. With the seam side down, start at one end and wrap the tenderloin with each strip of bacon. Top with freshly ground pepper. Carefully place the tenderloin seam side down on the prepared pan.

6. Roast for 40 to 50 minutes, depending on size of the tenderloin; the internal temperature should be 145°F. Turn the oven to the broil setting. Broil for 3 to 4 more minutes, until the bacon is as brown as you like.

7. Let the tenderloin rest for 15 minutes. Place on a serving platter and garnish with parsley, if desired.

NET CARBS 1.1g

calories	fat	protein	carbs	fiber
248	13.1g	29.9g	1.6g	0.5g

Slow Cooker Chipotle Shredded Beef

yield 12 servings • *prep time* 20 minutes • *cook time* 6 hours 20 minutes

2 tablespoons avocado oil

1 (3- to 4-pound) boneless beef chuck roast

Salt and pepper

1 medium onion, chopped

4 cloves garlic, minced

¼ cup apple cider vinegar

½ cup beef broth

1 (14½-ounce) can crushed tomatoes

1 tablespoon brown sugar substitute

2 teaspoons ground cumin

2 teaspoons ground dried oregano

1 teaspoon paprika

2 canned chipotle peppers in adobo sauce, finely chopped

1 tablespoon adobo sauce from the can

Fresh cilantro, for garnish (optional)

Serving suggestion:
2 recipes Cilantro Lime Coleslaw (page 240), or 4 cups cooked cauliflower rice

1. Heat the oil in a large heavy-bottomed skillet or pot over medium-high heat. Season the roast on all sides with salt and pepper. Sear the roast for 7 to 8 minutes on each side. Transfer the roast to a 6-quart slow cooker.

2. In the same skillet, cook the onion and garlic over medium heat until the onions are tender, about 5 minutes. Pour in the vinegar, broth, and tomatoes. Stir in the brown sugar substitute, cumin, oregano, paprika, 1 teaspoon of black pepper, chipotle peppers, and adobo sauce until well combined.

3. Slowly pour the onion mixture over the roast, making sure most of it remains on top of the roast. Place the lid on the slow cooker and cook on low heat until the beef easily shreds with a fork, 5 to 6 hours.

4. Use two forks to shred the beef in the slow cooker and mix with the juices. Garnish with cilantro and serve with coleslaw or rice, if desired.

Make Ahead

Can be made up to 3 days ahead. Store in an airtight container in the refrigerator. Reheat in the slow cooker using the warm setting.

	NET CARBS 3g			
calories	fat	protein	carbs	fiber
323	20.3g	30.6g	4.9g	2g

Bourbon BBQ Ribs

yield 8 servings • *prep time* 15 minutes, plus 1 hour to marinate (optional) • *cook time* 3½ hours

2 full racks St. Louis–style spareribs (about 3 pounds each)

2 tablespoons avocado oil

Rib seasoning:

2 teaspoons ground black pepper

1 teaspoon salt

½ teaspoon ground dried oregano

½ teaspoon smoked paprika

½ teaspoon garlic powder

½ teaspoon onion powder

BBQ sauce:

(Makes about 2½ cups)

1 cup tomato paste

1 cup water

½ cup bourbon

⅓ cup apple cider vinegar

¼ cup brown sugar substitute

2 tablespoons Worcestershire sauce

2 teaspoons chili powder

1 teaspoon smoked paprika

1 teaspoon salt

½ teaspoon ground black pepper

½ teaspoon garlic powder

1. Preheat the oven to 275°F. Grease or line a sheet pan with parchment paper or foil. (*Note:* If you plan to marinate the ribs, hold off on preheating the oven until ready to bake.)

2. Pat the ribs dry. Use a knife to remove the thin membrane from the back side of the ribs. Don't skip this step; it is necessary to ensure the ribs will be tender.

3. Brush the oil over both sides of the ribs. In a small mixing bowl, whisk together the ingredients for the rib seasoning. Sprinkle the seasoning evenly across the front and back of both racks of ribs, then use your hands to rub it in. Place the ribs bone side down on the prepared pan.

4. If you have time, place the ribs in the refrigerator to marinate for 1 hour or up to 6 hours. If not, skip to Step 5.

5. Place the ribs in the oven and bake for 3 hours.

6. While the ribs are baking, make the BBQ sauce: Bring the sauce ingredients to a boil in a medium-size saucepan over medium heat. Continue to boil, stirring continually, for 2 minutes. Reduce the heat to low and simmer gently, stirring occasionally, until the sauce has thickened slightly, 15 to 20 minutes. Remove the pan from the heat and allow the sauce to cool.

7. Remove the ribs from the oven and brush them liberally with the sauce. Bake for 30 more minutes, or until the meat is fall-off-the-bone tender. Remove from the oven, coat with more sauce, and let the ribs rest for 15 minutes before serving. Serve with extra sauce.

Note ————

If you don't care for the taste of bourbon, you can use the BBQ sauce on page 305 in place of this sauce.

Make Ahead ————

The sauce can be made up to 1 week ahead. The ribs can be prepped and marinated up to 6 hours ahead.

	NET CARBS 2.9g			
calories	fat	protein	carbs	fiber
401	33.3g	21.2g	3.9g	1g

Hawaiian Pull-Apart Rolls

yield 9 rolls (1 roll per serving) • *prep time* 15 minutes • *cook time* 25 minutes

2 cups finely shredded mozzarella cheese

2 ounces cream cheese (¼ cup)

1 tablespoon salted butter

¾ cup finely ground blanched almond flour

2 tablespoons coconut flour

2 tablespoons granular sweetener

2 teaspoons baking powder

1 teaspoon active dry yeast

1 large egg, whisked

1 teaspoon pure pineapple extract

1 large egg yolk, whisked, for brushing the rolls

Note —————

Unlike traditional yeasted rolls, this dough doesn't need to rise before being shaped and baked. Here, the yeast simply adds flavor.

1. Preheat the oven to 350°F. Grease the bottom and sides of an 11 by 7-inch baking pan with oil or line it with parchment paper across the bottom and up the sides.

2. Put the mozzarella, cream cheese, and butter in a large microwave-safe mixing bowl. Microwave on high for 90 seconds, stirring with a rubber spatula every 30 seconds. Remove from the microwave and stir until melted and smooth.

3. Add the flours, sweetener, baking powder, yeast, egg, and pineapple extract to the cheese mixture and stir to combine. Microwave for 10 seconds and stir again. Continue to mix the ingredients with the spatula until they're completely combined and a firm dough comes together.

4. Divide the dough into 9 equal portions. Roll each portion into a ball. Put the rolls in the pan (it's okay if they are close together). Brush the tops of the rolls with the whisked egg yolk. Bake for 22 to 25 minutes, until the rolls are golden brown. Allow the rolls to cool completely before removing them from the pan and pulling them apart to serve.

NET CARBS 1.3g				
calories	fat	protein	carbs	fiber
104	8.5g	5.7g	2.1g	0.8g

Cilantro Lime Coleslaw

yield 6 servings • *prep time* 15 minutes, plus 2 hours to chill

½ cup mayonnaise

½ cup sour cream

¼ cup freshly squeezed lime juice

½ cup chopped fresh cilantro, plus more for garnish if desired

¼ cup chopped red onions

2 cloves garlic, minced

1 teaspoon granular sweetener

½ teaspoon salt

½ teaspoon ground black pepper

1 (10-ounce) bag angel hair coleslaw (finely shredded green cabbage)

Lime wedges, for serving

1. In a medium-size serving bowl, whisk together the mayonnaise, sour cream, and lime juice. Stir in the cilantro, onions, garlic, sweetener, salt, and pepper until thoroughly combined.

2. Add the shredded cabbage to the bowl. Mix well and refrigerate for at least 2 hours before serving.

3. Garnish with cilantro, if desired, and serve with lime wedges.

Make Ahead

Can be made up to 1 day ahead. Store in an airtight container in the refrigerator.

	NET CARBS 3.8g			
calories	fat	protein	carbs	fiber
194	19.4g	1.5g	5.3g	1.4g

Roasted Garlic & Herb Breadsticks

yield 10 breadsticks (2 per serving) • *prep time* 20 minutes • *cook time* 1 hour

1 whole head garlic

1 teaspoon extra-virgin olive oil

1 cup shredded mozzarella cheese

½ cup grated Parmesan cheese

1 large egg

½ teaspoon ground dried oregano

½ teaspoon dried parsley

Low-sugar marinara sauce, for serving (optional)

Make Ahead

For the best flavor, the garlic can be roasted up to 2 days ahead. Store in an airtight container in the refrigerator.

1. Preheat the oven to 400°F.

2. Peel off the papery outer layer of the garlic. Use a knife to cut ¼ inch off the top of the head to expose the individual cloves. Drizzle the exposed cloves with the oil. Wrap the head in foil to create a pouch, closing it at the top.

3. Place the garlic on a sheet pan and roast until golden and soft, 40 to 45 minutes. Allow to cool.

4. Decrease the oven temperature to 375°F. Line a sheet pan with parchment paper.

5. In a medium-size mixing bowl, stir together the mozzarella, Parmesan, egg, oregano, parsley, and 4 cloves of the roasted garlic until well combined. (Save the rest of the garlic for other uses. You can store it in an airtight container in the refrigerator for up to 2 weeks.)

6. Use a rubber spatula to scoop the mixture onto the prepared pan. Use your hands to press the dough into a circle about 10 inches in diameter. Bake for 15 to 20 minutes, until the cheese has melted and the top and edges are lightly browned. Allow to cool for 10 minutes. Use a pizza cutter to cut into sticks. Serve with marinara sauce, if desired.

NET CARBS 3.1g

calories	fat	protein	carbs	fiber
133	8.7g	11.3g	3.3g	0.2g

Creamy Cucumber Salad

yield 6 servings • *prep time* 10 minutes, plus 2 hours to chill

1 large English cucumber

Salt

¼ cup sour cream

1 tablespoon white vinegar

1 tablespoon chopped fresh dill

½ teaspoon garlic powder

½ teaspoon ground black pepper

1. Slice the cucumber crosswise into thin rounds. Place the slices in a colander over the sink. Lightly sprinkle with salt and allow to sit for 10 minutes to draw out the excess moisture.

2. Use a paper towel to remove any remaining moisture from the cucumber slices, then transfer the cucumbers to a medium-size mixing bowl. Add the sour cream, vinegar, dill, garlic powder, pepper, and ½ teaspoon of salt and gently stir with a spoon.

3. Refrigerate the salad for 2 hours before serving.

Make Ahead

Can be made up to 1 day ahead. Store in an airtight container in the refrigerator. Stir before serving.

NET CARBS 1.1g

calories	fat	protein	carbs	fiber
25	1.7g	0.5g	1.3g	0.2g

Bacon Ranch Fauxtato Salad

yield 8 servings • *prep time* 20 minutes, plus 2 hours to chill • *cook time* 10 minutes

2 (10-ounce) bags frozen cauliflower florets

½ cup mayonnaise

½ cup sour cream

1½ teaspoons dried parsley

1 teaspoon dried dill weed

½ teaspoon garlic powder

½ teaspoon salt

½ teaspoon ground black pepper

2 green onions, sliced, plus more for garnish if desired

6 slices bacon, cooked and crumbled, plus more for garnish if desired

1. Cook the cauliflower according to the package directions. You want it to be very tender. Use a colander to drain the cauliflower and set aside to cool.

2. In a large mixing bowl, mix together the mayonnaise, sour cream, parsley, dill, garlic powder, salt, and pepper. Stir in the cauliflower, green onions, and bacon until well combined. Garnish with green onions and crumbled bacon, if desired.

3. Refrigerate the salad for at least 2 hours before serving.

Make Ahead

Can be made up to 1 day ahead. Store in an airtight container in the refrigerator.

		NET CARBS 2.5g		
calories	fat	protein	carbs	fiber
176	16.8g	4.5g	4.3g	1.8g

Okra Fritters

yield 8 fritters (1 per serving) • *prep time* 15 minutes • *cook time* 16 minutes

1½ cups finely ground blanched almond flour

1 teaspoon baking powder

½ teaspoon salt

½ teaspoon ground black pepper

¼ teaspoon cayenne pepper

2 cups sliced fresh okra

¼ cup chopped onions

1 large egg

¼ cup heavy whipping cream

¼ cup unsweetened almond milk

High-quality oil, for frying

1. In a medium-size mixing bowl, whisk together the almond flour, baking powder, salt, black pepper, and cayenne pepper. Add the okra and onions and toss to coat.

2. In a small mixing bowl, whisk together the egg, cream, and almond milk. Gently fold the okra mixture into the egg mixture until the okra is coated on all sides.

3. Pour ¼ inch of oil into a large skillet, then set the pan over medium heat and heat the oil until hot (when ready, it will appear to be shimmering). Working in a couple of batches, gently drop the batter in 2-tablespoon mounds into the pan. Fry until golden brown on both sides, about 4 minutes per side. Serve immediately. Repeat with the remaining batter, adding more oil to the pan after each batch. The fritters are best eaten hot, right out of the skillet.

NET CARBS 3.1g

calories	fat	protein	carbs	fiber
169	14.5g	5.9g	6.2g	3.2g

Mexican Cauli-Rice

yield 6 servings • *prep time* 10 minutes • *cook time* 22 minutes

2 tablespoons salted butter

¼ cup diced onions

1 clove garlic, minced

1 (12-ounce) bag frozen riced cauliflower

1 (10-ounce) can diced tomatoes and green chilies

1 teaspoon ground cumin

½ teaspoon chili powder

½ teaspoon salt

½ teaspoon ground black pepper

¼ teaspoon ground dried oregano

Finely chopped fresh cilantro, for garnish (optional)

1. Melt the butter in a medium-size skillet over medium heat. Cook the onions until tender, about 5 minutes. Add the garlic and cook for 1 more minute, until fragrant.

2. Put the cauliflower and diced tomatoes and green chilies in the skillet, then stir in the seasonings. Cook, stirring occasionally, until the rice is tender, about 15 minutes. Garnish with cilantro, if desired, and serve.

	NET CARBS 2.6g			
calories	fat	protein	carbs	fiber
60	3.9g	0.5g	4.8g	2.1g

Loaded Roasted Radishes

yield 6 servings • *prep time* 10 minutes • *cook time* 25 minutes

12 ounces radishes, trimmed and cut into bite-size pieces

2 tablespoons extra-virgin olive oil

½ teaspoon onion powder

½ teaspoon paprika

½ teaspoon dried parsley

¼ teaspoon ground dried oregano

½ teaspoon salt

½ teaspoon ground black pepper

6 slices bacon, diced

½ cup shredded cheddar cheese

Sliced green onions, for garnish (optional)

Ranch Dressing (page 302), for serving (optional)

1. Preheat the oven to 425°F. Line a sheet pan with parchment paper.

2. In a medium-size mixing bowl, toss the radishes with the oil until coated. Sprinkle with the onion powder, paprika, parsley, oregano, salt, and pepper and stir until the radishes are evenly coated in the seasonings.

3. Spread the radishes on the prepared pan and evenly top them with the bacon. Roast for 20 minutes. Remove from the oven and evenly sprinkle the cheese on the radishes. Bake for 2 to 4 more minutes, until the cheese has melted.

4. If desired, garnish with green onion slices and serve with ranch dressing. Best eaten the same day.

NET CARBS 1.3g

calories	fat	protein	carbs	fiber
142	12.1g	5.9g	2.4g	1.1g

Maple Bourbon Brussels Sprouts

yield 6 servings • *prep time* 10 minutes • *cook time* 35 minutes

1 pound Brussels sprouts, trimmed and cut in half

2 slices bacon, chopped

1 tablespoon avocado oil

Glaze:

2 tablespoons sugar-free maple syrup

1 teaspoon bourbon

1 teaspoon granular sweetener

½ teaspoon salt

¼ teaspoon ground black pepper

1. Preheat the oven to 400°F. Line a sheet pan with parchment paper.

2. In a medium-size mixing bowl, toss the Brussels sprouts and bacon with the oil. Spread the mixture on the prepared pan in an even layer. Roast for 15 minutes.

3. Meanwhile, prepare the glaze: In a small mixing bowl, whisk together the maple syrup, bourbon, sweetener, salt, and pepper. Drizzle the Brussels sprouts with the glaze and roast for an additional 15 to 20 minutes, until they are tender and as crispy as you like them. Serve immediately. Best eaten the same day.

NET CARBS 4.3g

calories	fat	protein	carbs	fiber
82	4.1g	3.7g	11.8g	7.6g

Green Bean Casserole with Fried Onions

yield 6 servings • *prep time* 20 minutes • *cook time* 40 minutes

High-quality oil, for frying

½ cup unsweetened almond milk

1 teaspoon white vinegar

½ cup whey protein powder (unflavored and unsweetened)

½ teaspoon garlic powder

1 teaspoon salt, divided

¼ teaspoon cayenne pepper

¼ teaspoon paprika

1 medium onion, thinly sliced

½ cup sour cream

¼ cup mayonnaise

2 teaspoons Worcestershire sauce

½ teaspoon ground black pepper

¼ teaspoon onion powder

2 (14½-ounce) cans Italian green beans, drained

1. Heat ½ inch of oil in a large deep skillet over medium heat.

2. While the oil is heating, whisk together the almond milk and vinegar in a shallow dish. In a separate shallow dish, whisk together the whey protein, garlic powder, ½ teaspoon of the salt, cayenne pepper, and paprika.

3. Dip a few onions at a time in the almond milk mixture, allowing the excess to drip back into the bowl, then coat them in the whey protein mixture. Repeat until all of the onion slices are coated. (*Tip:* Use tongs or a fork because whey breading tends to be stickier than breading made with regular flour.)

4. Preheat the oven to 350°F. Grease an 11 by 7-inch baking dish with oil.

5. Place a single layer of breaded onion slices in the hot oil, leaving space between them. Fry until golden brown on both sides, 3 to 4 minutes per side. Drain on a paper towel-lined plate. Repeat with the remaining breaded onion slices, adding more oil to the pan if needed.

6. In a medium-size mixing bowl, stir together the sour cream, mayonnaise, Worcestershire sauce, remaining ½ teaspoon of salt, black pepper, and onion powder. Gently fold in the green beans until well combined.

7. Transfer the green bean mixture to the prepared baking dish. Sprinkle the casserole evenly with the fried onions. Bake for 25 minutes, or until bubbly around the edges. Best eaten the same day.

	NET CARBS 5.4g			
calories	fat	protein	carbs	fiber
192	11.6g	14.2g	7.5g	2g

Roasted Veggie Skewers

yield 6 servings • *prep time* 15 minutes • *cook time* 25 minutes

2 tablespoons avocado oil

½ teaspoon salt

½ teaspoon ground black pepper

¼ teaspoon garlic powder

¼ teaspoon ground dried oregano

12 ounces radishes, trimmed

1 medium zucchini, cut into 1½-inch chunks

1 medium yellow squash, cut into 1½-inch chunks

1 medium red onion, cut into 1½-inch chunks

8 ounces medium white mushrooms

Special equipment: 6 (10-inch) wood skewers, soaked in water for 20 minutes

1. Preheat the oven to 425°F. Line a sheet pan with parchment paper.

2. In a small mixing bowl, whisk together the oil, salt, pepper, garlic powder, and oregano.

3. Thread the vegetables onto the skewers as you like. Set them on the prepared pan and brush them with the oil mixture, coating all sides. Let sit for 10 minutes.

4. Roast the skewers for 22 to 25 minutes, until tender, turning them halfway through. Serve immediately. Best eaten the same day.

Make Ahead

To streamline cooking on the day of the gathering, clean and trim and/or cut all of the vegetables the day before.

	NET CARBS 4.6g			
calories	fat	protein	carbs	fiber
79	5g	2.6g	7.2g	2.6g

CHAPTER 7

Desserts

Lemon Ricotta Cookies

yield About 30 cookies (2 per serving) • *prep time* 15 minutes, plus 1 hour to chill dough • *cook time* 14 minutes

1¾ cups finely ground blanched almond flour

2 tablespoons coconut flour

2 teaspoons baking powder

¼ teaspoon salt

1 (15-ounce) container ricotta cheese, well drained

1 large egg

¾ cup granular sweetener

Grated zest of 1 lemon, plus more for garnish if desired

2 tablespoons freshly squeezed lemon juice

½ teaspoon pure vanilla extract

Glaze:

¾ cup confectioners' sweetener

Grated zest and juice of 1 lemon

Make Ahead

The dough can be made up to 1 day ahead; cover tightly and store in the refrigerator. The cookies can also be made up to 1 day ahead; store in an airtight container on the counter.

1. In a medium-size mixing bowl, whisk together the flours, baking powder, and salt.

2. In a large mixing bowl, use a rubber spatula to stir together the ricotta, egg, granular sweetener, and lemon zest until mostly smooth, using the spatula to smash the ingredients against the side of the bowl. Stir in the lemon juice and vanilla until well combined.

3. Stir the flour mixture into the ricotta mixture a little at a time until well combined, but don't overmix.

4. Cover the dough and place it in the refrigerator to chill for at least 1 hour.

5. Preheat the oven to 350°F. Line a baking sheet with parchment paper.

6. Using a 1-tablespoon cookie scoop, scoop up the dough and place on the prepared baking sheet, spacing the cookies about 2 inches apart.

7. Bake for 13 to 14 minutes, until the bottoms are slightly golden. The tops of the cookies will be set but light in color. Allow the cookies to cool completely on the baking sheet; they are fragile when they are hot.

8. To make the glaze, place the sweetener, zest, and juice in a small mixing bowl and whisk until smooth. Drizzle the glaze over the tops of the cookies. Garnish with more lemon zest, if desired.

NET CARBS 1.8g				
calories	fat	protein	carbs	fiber
107	8.6g	4.5g	3.6g	1.8g

Cake Pops

yield About 16 cake pops (1 per serving) • *prep time* 40 minutes, plus 2 hours to chill • *cook time* 30 minutes

Cake:

1 cup finely ground blanched almond flour

1 tablespoon coconut flour

1½ teaspoons baking powder

¼ teaspoon xanthan gum

¼ teaspoon salt

5 tablespoons salted butter, softened

½ cup granular sweetener

2 large eggs

2 teaspoons pure vanilla extract

2 tablespoons heavy whipping cream

Frosting:

6 tablespoons unsalted butter, softened

½ cup confectioners' sweetener

1 to 2 teaspoons heavy whipping cream

Coating:

¾ cup sugar-free white chocolate chips

¾ cup sugar-free milk chocolate chips

¼ cup sugar-free rainbow sprinkles

Special equipment:

16 lollipop sticks

NET CARBS 3.2g				
calories	fat	protein	carbs	fiber
202	18.4g	3.7g	8.8g	5.7g

1. Preheat the oven to 350°F. Grease a 9-inch round cake pan with butter or avocado oil spray.

2. In a medium-size mixing bowl, whisk together the flours, baking powder, xanthan gum, and salt.

3. In a separate medium-size mixing bowl, use a hand mixer on medium speed to cream the butter and granular sweetener until fluffy. Beat in the eggs one at a time. Blend in the vanilla and cream.

4. With the mixer on low speed, add the flour mixture to the butter mixture a little at a time, mixing until the ingredients are incorporated. Spread the batter evenly in the prepared pan and smooth the top.

5. Bake for 25 to 30 minutes, until a toothpick or cake tester comes out clean. Set the pan on a wire rack and allow the cake to cool completely.

6. Meanwhile, make the frosting: In a medium-size mixing bowl, use the hand mixer on medium speed to cream the butter and confectioners' sweetener until smooth. Scrape down the sides of the bowl. Beat in the cream 1 teaspoon at a time until the frosting is light and fluffy and has the consistency of buttercream.

7. Crumble the cake into a large mixing bowl. Transfer the frosting to the bowl with the cake crumbles and stir until well combined.

8. Line a sheet pan with parchment paper. Scoop 1 tablespoon of the cake mixture and use your hands to roll it into a ball. Repeat with the rest of the cake mixture, placing the balls on the lined pan. Refrigerate for 2 hours. Reroll the chilled balls to smooth them out if needed.

9. In a small microwave-safe bowl, melt the white chocolate in the microwave on high in 30-second increments, stirring between increments. Be careful not burn the chocolate. Repeat with the milk chocolate chips using a separate bowl.

10. Line a sheet pan with parchment paper. Dip the end of a lollipop stick about ½ inch into the melted milk or white chocolate, then insert the coated end of the stick into the center of a cake ball. Push the stick about halfway in. Use the stick to dip the cake ball into the melted chocolate until it is completely coated. Allow the excess chocolate to drip off. Place the cake pop on the parchment paper and immediately decorate with sprinkles before the chocolate hardens. Repeat with the remaining cake balls, melted chocolate, and sprinkles. (*Note:* If the melted chocolate starts to harden, reheat it briefly in the microwave.) Refrigerate the cake pops for 15 minutes to set the chocolate.

Make Ahead

Can be made up to 3 days ahead. Store in an airtight container in the refrigerator. Set the cake pops out 30 minutes before serving.

No-Bake Cheesecake Cups

yield 6 servings • *prep time* 10 minutes, plus 2 hours to chill

1 (8-ounce) package cream cheese, softened

½ cup confectioners' sweetener

1 cup heavy whipping cream

1 teaspoon pure vanilla extract

Berries of choice, for garnish

Special equipment: 6 (8-ounce) clear serving cups

1. In a medium-size mixing bowl, use a hand mixer on medium speed to mix the cream cheese and sweetener until smooth. Pour the cream and vanilla into the bowl and mix until smooth and creamy.

2. Divide the mixture evenly among the serving cups. Cover the cups and refrigerate for at least 2 hours before serving. Garnish each serving with berries.

Make Ahead

Can be made up to 3 days ahead. Store covered in the refrigerator.

	NET CARBS 0.8g			
calories	fat	protein	carbs	fiber
249	27g	2.7g	0.8g	0g

Tiramisu Mousse

yield 6 servings • *prep time* 10 minutes (not including time to make whipped cream), plus 1 hour to chill

1 (8-ounce) container mascarpone cheese

½ cup confectioners' sweetener

1 tablespoon cocoa powder

2 tablespoons cold espresso or strong brewed coffee

1 teaspoon pure vanilla extract

1 cup heavy whipping cream

For garnish:
1 cup Whipped Cream (page 296)

Cocoa powder

1. Place the mascarpone and sweetener in a medium-size mixing bowl. Use a hand mixer on medium speed to blend until smooth.

2. With the mixer still on medium speed, mix in the cocoa powder, espresso, and vanilla. Scrape down the sides of the bowl. Pour in the cream and continue mixing until smooth and creamy.

3. Transfer the mousse to six 8-ounce serving bowls and refrigerate for at least 1 hour before serving. Garnish each serving with a dollop of whipped cream and a dusting of cocoa powder. For a fancier presentation, pipe the whipped cream on top.

Make Ahead

The mousse can be made up to 1 day ahead. Store covered in the refrigerator. Add the whipped cream and dusting of cocoa powder before serving.

NET CARBS 0.4g

calories	fat	protein	carbs	fiber
280	32.5g	2.9g	0.6g	0.2g

Dad's Strawberry Fluff Salad

yield 8 servings • *prep time* 15 minutes, plus 2 hours to chill

1½ cups heavy whipping cream

¼ cup granular sweetener

½ teaspoon pure vanilla extract

1 (16-ounce) container small curd cottage cheese

1 (0.3-ounce) package strawberry-flavored sugar-free gelatin

1 cup sliced strawberries

Suggested garnishes:
Whipped Cream (page 296)
Whole strawberries

1. Place the cream, sweetener, and vanilla in a large mixing bowl. Use a hand mixer to beat on high speed until stiff peaks form.

2. In a medium-size mixing bowl, stir together the cottage cheese and gelatin until combined. Gently fold the sweetened whipped cream into the cottage cheese mixture until combined, making sure not to overmix. Gently fold in the strawberries.

3. Transfer to a serving bowl, cover, and refrigerate for at least 2 hours before serving. Garnish with whipped cream and strawberries, if desired.

Note

When developing recipes, I often use my family and friends as taste testers. My dad loved this recipe so much that my mom started making it for him on a regular basis. I guess you could say it's a winner! Naturally I thought it should be named after him.

Make Ahead

Can be made up to 1 day ahead. Store covered in the refrigerator. Garnish with whipped cream and strawberries, if desired, right before serving.

NET CARBS 2.7g

calories	fat	protein	carbs	fiber
189	17.7g	7.2g	3.1g	0.4g

Creamy Vanilla Yogurt Fruit Dip

yield 8 servings • *prep time* 10 minutes

1 (8-ounce) package cream cheese, softened

½ cup confectioners' sweetener

1½ cups low-carb vanilla yogurt

Assorted berries, for serving

Special equipment (optional):
Cocktail toothpicks, for serving

In a medium-size mixing bowl, use a hand mixer on medium speed to mix the cream cheese and sweetener until smooth. Mix in the yogurt until smooth and creamy. Serve with berries for dipping.

Notes

There are several brands of yogurt that would be acceptable for this recipe. Look for the one with the lowest carbs. I used Two Good for the recipes in this book.

The nutrition information below is for the dip only.

Make Ahead

Can be made up to 2 days ahead. Store in an airtight container in the refrigerator.

	NET CARBS	1.4g		
calories	fat	protein	carbs	fiber
124	10.7g	5.4g	1.4g	0g

Chocolate Cream Cheese Dip

yield 8 servings • *prep time* 15 minutes, plus 1 hour to chill

1 (8-ounce) package cream cheese, softened

¼ cup granular sweetener

1 teaspoon pure vanilla extract

½ cup heavy whipping cream

½ cup sugar-free milk or dark chocolate chips, plus more for garnish if desired

Berries of choice, for serving

Special equipment (optional):
Cocktail toothpicks, for serving

1. Place the cream cheese, sweetener, and vanilla in a medium-size mixing bowl and use a hand mixer on medium speed to mix until smooth and creamy.

2. In a small microwave-safe mixing bowl, microwave the cream on high in 30-second increments until hot but not boiling. Add the chocolate chips to the hot cream and let sit for 2 minutes, or until the chips are melted. Whisk until smooth.

3. Fold the chocolate-flavored cream into the cream cheese mixture until well combined. Cover and refrigerate for at least 1 hour before serving. Garnish with chocolate chips, if desired, and serve with berries for dipping.

Make Ahead

Can be made up to 2 days ahead. Store in an airtight container in the refrigerator.

NET CARBS 2.2g

calories	fat	protein	carbs	fiber
189	18.4g	2.8g	5.4g	3.2g

Strawberry Cobbler

yield 6 servings • *prep time* 15 minutes • *cook time* 40 minutes

2 tablespoons salted butter

1 cup finely ground blanched almond flour

¾ cup granular sweetener, divided

1 tablespoon baking powder

¼ teaspoon salt

½ cup heavy whipping cream

1 teaspoon pure vanilla extract

1½ cups sliced strawberries

¼ cup very hot water

1. Preheat the oven to 350°F. Put the butter in an 11 by 7-inch baking dish and place the dish in the oven to melt the butter.

2. In a medium-size mixing bowl, whisk together the almond flour, ½ cup of the sweetener, the baking powder, and salt. Add the cream and vanilla and stir until well combined.

3. Remove the baking dish from the oven and tilt the dish to ensure the butter evenly covers the bottom, all the way to the edges. Pour the batter on top of the melted butter in the dish and gently spread it to the edges.

4. Top the batter with the strawberries and remaining ¼ cup of sweetener. Pour the hot water evenly over the cobbler. Do not stir. Bake for 30 to 40 minutes, until the top is light golden brown and the edges are caramelized.

Note ————

This is delicious served with whipped cream (page 296) or low-carb vanilla ice cream (see page 290 for my recipe).

NET CARBS 4.3g

calories	fat	protein	carbs	fiber
221	20.7g	4.3g	7.1g	2.8g

Double Chocolate Bundt Cake

yield 12 servings • *prep time* 20 minutes • *cook time* 45 minutes

2 cups finely ground blanched almond flour

⅓ cup cocoa powder

2 teaspoons baking powder

1 teaspoon baking soda

½ teaspoon xanthan gum

¼ teaspoon salt

½ cup (1 stick) salted butter, softened

1 cup granular sweetener

3 large eggs

1 teaspoon pure vanilla extract

1 cup sour cream

½ cup very hot brewed coffee

½ cup sugar-free semi-sweet chocolate chips

Ganache:

⅓ cup heavy whipping cream

½ cup sugar-free semi-sweet chocolate chips

Make Ahead

Can be made up to 1 day ahead. Store in a cake storage container on the counter. Be sure the container doesn't touch the ganache topping. Alternatively, bake the cake the day before and make the ganache and drizzle it over the cake shortly before serving.

1. Preheat the oven to 350°F. Grease or spray a 12-cup Bundt pan with oil.

2. In a medium-size mixing bowl, whisk together the almond flour, cocoa powder, baking powder, baking soda, xanthan gum, and salt.

3. In a large mixing bowl, use a hand mixer on medium speed to cream the butter and sweetener until light and fluffy. Scrape down the sides of the bowl, then add the eggs one at a time, mixing well and scraping down the sides after each addition. Blend in the vanilla. With the mixer running on low speed, add the almond flour mixture and sour cream a little at a time, alternating between them. Once the wet and dry ingredients are blended, turn off the mixer and stir in the hot coffee until just combined. Gently fold the chocolate chips into the batter.

4. Spoon the batter into the prepared Bundt pan. Gently tap the pan on the counter to release any air bubbles. Smooth the top with the back of a spoon. Bake for 40 to 45 minutes, until a toothpick or cake tester inserted in the center comes out with just a few crumbs on it.

5. Remove the cake from the oven and allow to cool on a wire rack for 10 to 15 minutes. Gently run a knife around the edge of the pan to loosen the sides and invert the cake onto a cake stand or plate. Allow to finish cooling.

6. To make the ganache, heat the cream in a small saucepan over medium heat until it starts to simmer. Remove the pan from the heat and add the chocolate chips to the cream. Let sit for 5 minutes, then whisk the cream and chocolate chips together until smooth and glossy. Drizzle the ganache evenly over the top of the cake, allowing it run down the sides. Let the ganache firm up before slicing and serving.

NET CARBS 5.6g

calories	fat	protein	carbs	fiber
369	32.7g	7.6g	12g	6.4g

Better-Than-Anything Cake

yield 20 servings • *prep time* 30 minutes (not including time to make caramel sauce or whipped cream), plus at least 8 hours to chill • *cook time* 45 minutes

2 cups finely ground blanched almond flour

⅓ cup cocoa powder

2 teaspoons baking powder

1 teaspoon baking soda

½ teaspoon xanthan gum

¼ teaspoon salt

½ cup (1 stick) salted butter, softened, plus more for greasing the pan

1 cup granular sweetener

3 large eggs

1 teaspoon pure vanilla extract

½ cup very hot water

½ cup sugar-free milk chocolate chips

¾ cup Caramel Sauce (page 292)

1 recipe Whipped Cream (page 296)

3 ounces sugar-free candy bar, chopped, for garnish

Note ————

I used a Lily's Salted Almond Milk Chocolate Style candy bar for the topping.

Make Ahead ————

Can be made up to 2 days ahead. Store covered in the refrigerator.

1. Preheat the oven to 350°F. Grease a 13 by 9-inch cake pan with butter.

2. In a medium-size mixing bowl, whisk together the almond flour, cocoa powder, baking powder, baking soda, xanthan gum, and salt.

3. In a large mixing bowl, use a hand mixer on medium speed to cream the butter and sweetener until light and fluffy. Scrape down the sides of the bowl. Mix in the eggs one at a time, scraping down the sides after each addition. Mix in the vanilla.

4. With the mixer on low speed, add the flour mixture to the butter mixture a little at a time until incorporated. Pour in the hot water and stir until just combined. Gently fold the chocolate chips into the batter.

5. Spoon the batter into the prepared cake pan and smooth the top with the back of a spoon.

6. Bake the cake for 40 to 45 minutes, until a toothpick or cake tester inserted in the center of the cake comes out clean.

7. Remove the cake from the oven and use the handle of a wooden spoon to poke holes at 1-inch intervals throughout the top of the cake.

8. Pour the caramel sauce evenly over the top of the cake. Allow to finish cooling.

9. Once the cake has completely cooled, spread the whipped cream evenly over the top of the cake. Garnish with the chopped candy bar. Cover and refrigerate the cake for at least 8 hours or overnight before slicing and serving.

	NET CARBS	2.1g		
calories	fat	protein	carbs	fiber
252	25.7g	4.1g	5.3g	3.2g

Turtle Pie

yield 10 servings • *prep time* 30 minutes (not including time to make caramel sauce),
plus 2 hours to chill • *cook time* 14 minutes

Pie crust:

1½ cups finely ground blanched almond flour

¼ cup (½ stick) salted butter, softened, plus more for greasing the pie plate

2 tablespoons brown sugar substitute

½ teaspoon pure vanilla extract

⅛ teaspoon salt

Filling:

1 (8-ounce) package cream cheese, softened

½ cup confectioners' sweetener

1 cup heavy whipping cream

1 teaspoon pure vanilla extract

½ cup Caramel Sauce (page 292), cooled, divided

2 tablespoons sugar-free semi-sweet chocolate chips

2 tablespoons chopped raw pecans

1. Preheat the oven to 350°F. Grease a 9-inch pie plate with butter.

2. In a medium-size mixing bowl, whisk together the ingredients for the pie crust until the mixture resembles coarse crumbs.

3. Transfer the dough to the prepared pie plate. Using your hands, evenly press the dough across the bottom and up the sides of the plate. Use a fork to lightly prick the crust several times.

4. Bake the crust for 12 to 14 minutes, until light golden brown. Allow to cool.

5. While the crust cools, prepare the filling: In a medium-size mixing bowl, use a hand mixer on medium speed to mix the cream cheese and sweetener until smooth. Mix in the cream and vanilla until the filling is smooth and creamy.

6. Spread ¼ cup of the caramel sauce evenly across the cooled pie crust. Carefully pour the filling on top of the caramel, spreading it to the edges and smoothing the top. Pour the rest of the caramel sauce on top of the pie and spread it into an even layer. Sprinkle the chocolate chips and chopped pecans on top. Refrigerate the pie for at least 2 hours before slicing and serving.

Make Ahead

Can be made up to 2 days ahead. Store covered in the refrigerator.

	NET CARBS 2.1g			
calories	fat	protein	carbs	fiber
461	48.8g	5.7g	4.7g	2.6g

Pecan Pumpkin Crisp

yield 8 servings • *prep time* 15 minutes • *cook time* 45 minutes

2 large eggs

½ cup granular sweetener

1 (15-ounce) can pumpkin puree

⅔ cup heavy whipping cream

1 teaspoon pure vanilla extract

2 teaspoons pumpkin pie spice

¼ teaspoon salt

Crumble topping:

½ cup chopped raw pecans

¼ cup (½ stick) salted butter, softened

¼ cup finely ground blanched almond flour

¼ cup brown sugar substitute

½ teaspoon ground cinnamon

1. Preheat the oven to 375°F. Grease a 10-inch cast-iron skillet or 9-inch square baking dish with oil.

2. In a medium-size mixing bowl, whisk together the eggs and sweetener until smooth. Stir in the pumpkin puree, cream, vanilla, pumpkin pie spice, and salt until well blended. Pour the mixture into the prepared skillet.

3. Place all of the crumble topping ingredients in a small mixing bowl and use a fork to combine them until the mixture has a crumbly texture. Sprinkle the crumble mixture evenly over the pumpkin filling.

4. Cover the pan with foil and bake for 20 minutes. Remove the foil and bake for an additional 20 to 25 minutes, until the pumpkin filling is set and the crumble topping is golden brown.

Note

The crisp can be served with whipped cream (page 296) or low-carb vanilla ice cream (see my recipe on page 290).

NET CARBS 3.9g

calories	fat	protein	carbs	fiber
162	14.1g	3.5g	6.3g	2.5g

Strawberry Shortcake Trifle

yield 10 servings • *prep time* 20 minutes (not including time to make whipped cream), plus 4 hours to chill • *cook time* 15 minutes

1 (16-ounce) container strawberries, sliced

2 tablespoons granular sweetener

Shortcakes:

1 cup finely ground blanched almond flour

2 tablespoons coconut flour

⅓ cup granular sweetener

2 teaspoons baking powder

⅛ teaspoon salt

2 large eggs

2 tablespoons heavy whipping cream

2 tablespoons salted butter, melted and cooled slightly

1 teaspoon pure vanilla extract

Cream cheese filling:

12 ounces cream cheese, softened

½ cup confectioners' sweetener

1½ cups heavy whipping cream

1 teaspoon pure vanilla extract

1 cup Whipped Cream (page 296), for the top

Special equipment: **Trifle bowl and piping bag with star tip (see Note, opposite)**

1. Place the strawberry slices in a medium-size mixing bowl. Sprinkle with the granular sweetener. Gently stir and set aside to macerate.

2. Preheat the oven to 375°F. Line a baking sheet with parchment paper.

3. To make the shortcakes, whisk together the almond flour, coconut flour, granular sweetener, baking powder, and salt in a small mixing bowl.

4. In a medium-size mixing bowl, whisk the eggs, then whisk in the cream, cooled melted butter, and vanilla. Slowly add the flour mixture, stirring until well blended.

5. Drop 2-ounce scoops of the batter onto the prepared baking sheet, spacing the shortcakes 2 inches apart, to make a total of 8 shortcakes. Bake for 13 to 15 minutes, until the tops of the shortcakes are golden brown and a toothpick or cake tester inserted in the middle of a cake comes out clean. Allow to cool completely on the pan.

6. While the shortcakes bake, make the filling: In a medium-size mixing bowl, use a hand mixer on medium speed to beat the cream cheese and confectioners' sweetener until creamy. Slowly mix in the cream and vanilla and continue to beat until the mixture is light and fluffy.

7. To assemble the trifle, cut the shortcakes in half horizontally. Place 8 halves in the bottom of the trifle bowl. Evenly layer half of the macerated strawberries on top of the shortcakes. Spread half of the cream cheese mixture over the strawberries. Layer the remaining shortcake halves on top of the cream cheese mixture, followed by the rest of the strawberries. Cover and refrigerate the trifle for at least 4 hours.

8. Using a piping bag and tip, decorate the top of the trifle with the whipped cream before serving.

NET CARBS 4.5g

calories	fat	protein	carbs	fiber
358	34.9g	6.7g	6.9g	2.4g

Note

If you don't have a trifle mixing bowl, you can use a large straight-sided clear glass vase or simply a large clear glass mixing bowl. If you have a whipped cream dispenser (see the note on page 59), you can save yourself the step of whipping the cream by hand, and there's no need for a piping bag and tip!

Make Ahead

Can be made up to 1 day ahead. Store covered in the refrigerator. Add the whipped cream right before serving.

Birthday Cake Granola

yield 3 cups (¼ cup per serving) • *prep time* 5 minutes • *cook time* 25 minutes

1 cup chopped raw pecans

1 cup roasted and salted shelled sunflower seeds

½ cup sliced almonds

1 large egg white

2 tablespoons granular sweetener

2 tablespoons salted butter, melted and cooled slightly

2 teaspoons pure vanilla extract

½ cup sugar-free white chocolate chips

¼ cup sugar-free rainbow sprinkles

1. Preheat the oven to 325°F. Line a sheet pan with parchment paper.

2. In a medium-size mixing bowl, stir together the pecans, sunflower seeds, and almonds.

3. In a small mixing bowl, whisk the egg white until frothy, then stir in the sweetener, cooled melted butter, and vanilla. Pour the egg white mixture over the nut mixture and stir until completely coated.

4. Spread the granola in an even layer on the prepared pan. Bake for 20 to 25 minutes, stirring every 10 minutes, until light golden brown. Immediately sprinkle the white chocolate chips and sprinkles evenly over the top of the granola. Allow to cool completely before serving.

Make Ahead

Can be made up to 1 week ahead. Store in an airtight container in the refrigerator.

	NET CARBS 1.4g			
calories	fat	protein	carbs	fiber
161	15g	4g	4.4g	3g

Vanilla Ice Cream

yield 1 quart (½ cup per serving) • *prep time* 5 minutes, plus 2 hours to chill base and time to churn

2 cups heavy whipping cream

1 cup unsweetened almond milk

½ cup granular allulose

1 teaspoon pure vanilla extract

Pinch of salt

Special equipment: Ice cream maker

1. In a medium-size mixing bowl, whisk together the cream, almond milk, and allulose until the allulose is dissolved. Whisk in the vanilla and salt. Cover and refrigerate the mixture for 2 hours.

2. Stir the mixture and pour into the frozen ice cream mixing bowl. Churn the ice cream according to the manufacturer's instructions until it has the consistency of soft serve.

3. Serve immediately or scoop the ice cream into a lidded container and freeze until ready to serve.

Notes

Allulose is necessary for this recipe to keep the ice cream soft for scooping. Other sugar-free sweeteners tend to make the ice cream too hard to scoop. Remember to place the mixing bowl of your ice cream maker in the freezer 24 hours before you plan to make the ice cream.

Set up an ice cream sundae bar for a special celebration! Pair this ice cream with Caramel Sauce (page 292), Hot Fudge Sauce (page 294), Birthday Cake Granola (page 288), whipped cream (page 296), sugar-free chocolate chips, and fresh berries.

Make Ahead

Can be made up to 2 days ahead. Allow to sit on the counter for 10 minutes before serving.

	NET CARBS 0.2g			
calories	fat	protein	carbs	fiber
174	20.6g	0.2g	0.3g	0.1g

Caramel Sauce

yield 1 cup (2 tablespoons per serving) • *prep time* 5 minutes • *cook time* 10 minutes

¼ cup (½ stick) salted butter, cubed

½ cup granular allulose

1 cup heavy whipping cream

½ teaspoon pure vanilla extract

Pinch of salt

1. Melt the butter in a medium-size heavy-bottomed saucepan over medium heat. Stir in the allulose and bring to a low simmer. While gently whisking, slowly pour in the cream. Continue cooking, stirring constantly, until the caramel starts to thicken and turn golden brown.

2. Remove the caramel from the heat and stir in the vanilla and salt.

3. Allow to cool for 10 minutes before transferring to a heat-proof lidded container. The caramel will continue to thicken as it cools. Do not cover the container until the caramel sauce has completely cooled.

Note

Allulose is the best sweetener for this recipe because it will keep the caramel smooth and will not crystallize when cooled.

Make Ahead

The sauce can be made up to 3 days ahead. Allow to cool completely before storing in a jar in the refrigerator. When ready to use, reheat in a saucepan over low heat.

NET CARBS 0g

calories	fat	protein	carbs	fiber
136	15.9g	0.1g	0g	0g

Hot Fudge Sauce

yield 1½ cups (2 tablespoons per serving) • *prep time* 5 minutes • *cook time* 10 minutes

½ cup (1 stick) salted butter, cubed

1 cup heavy whipping cream

⅔ cup granular allulose

¾ cup cocoa powder

1 teaspoon pure vanilla extract

Pinch of salt

1. Heat the butter, cream, and allulose in a medium-size heavy-bottomed saucepan over medium heat. Stir frequently until the butter melts and the mixture starts to simmer. Reduce the heat to low.

2. Whisk in the cocoa powder a little at time so it doesn't clump. Continue to cook until the hot fudge starts to thicken and become glossy. Stir in the salt.

3. Allow the hot fudge to cool for 10 minutes before serving.

Note

I like to use Hershey's Special Dark cocoa powder for this sauce. Being Dutched (aka Dutch-processed), it makes an extra dark and rich hot fudge! But any cocoa powder will do. Don't miss my homemade vanilla ice cream recipe on page 290—it's the perfect pairing for this sauce!

Make Ahead

Can be made up to 3 days ahead. Allow to cool completely before storing in a jar in the refrigerator. When ready to use, reheat in a saucepan over low heat.

NET CARBS 1g

calories	fat	protein	carbs	fiber
136	15.1g	1g	2.8g	1.8g

Whipped Cream

yield 2 cups (¼ cup per serving) • *prep time* 5 minutes

1 cup heavy whipping cream

¼ cup granular sweetener

1 teaspoon pure vanilla extract

Place the cream, sweetener, and vanilla in the bowl of a stand mixer, or use a hand mixer and a large mixing bowl. Mix on high speed until stiff peaks form.

NET CARBS 1.6g

calories	fat	protein	carbs	fiber
220	22.8g	1.1g	1.6g	0g

CHAPTER 8

Basics

Taco Seasoning

yield about ½ cup (1 tablespoon per serving) • *prep time* 5 minutes

¼ cup chili powder

2 tablespoons ground cumin

1 tablespoon smoked paprika

2 teaspoons salt

1 teaspoon ground black pepper

1 teaspoon garlic powder

1 teaspoon onion powder

1 teaspoon ground dried oregano

In a small mixing bowl, stir the ingredients together until well combined. Store in a jar with a lid. Shake before use.

Note

Use 2 tablespoons of taco seasoning per pound of meat.

NET CARBS 1.2g

calories	fat	protein	carbs	fiber
10	0g	0.5g	1.8g	0.6g

Ranch Seasoning

yield about 1 cup (1 tablespoon per serving) • *prep time* 5 minutes

5 tablespoons dried parsley

3 tablespoons dried dill weed

2 tablespoons dried chives

2 tablespoons garlic powder

1 tablespoon dried minced onions

1 tablespoon onion powder

2 teaspoons salt

2 teaspoons ground black pepper

In a small mixing bowl, stir the ingredients together until well combined. Store in a jar with a lid. Shake before use.

	NET CARBS 1.6g			
calories	fat	protein	carbs	fiber
9	0.1g	0.5g	2g	0.4g

Ranch Dressing

yield about 2 cups (¼ cup per serving) • *prep time* 5 minutes (not including time to make seasoning)

1 cup sour cream

½ cup mayonnaise

¼ cup heavy whipping cream, plus more if needed

1 teaspoon freshly squeezed lemon juice

2 tablespoons Ranch Seasoning (page 301)

In a small mixing bowl, stir all of the ingredients together until well blended. If the dressing is too thick, thin it with more cream, adding 1 teaspoon at a time.

Make Ahead

Can be made up to 1 week ahead. Store in an airtight container in the refrigerator.

NET CARBS 0.9g

calories	fat	protein	carbs	fiber
148	15.4g	0.6g	1g	0.1g

Blue Cheese Dressing

yield about 2 cups (¼ cup per serving) • *prep time* 5 minutes

1 cup crumbled blue cheese

½ cup mayonnaise

¼ cup heavy whipping cream

¼ cup sour cream

1 tablespoon chopped fresh chives

1 teaspoon freshly squeezed lemon juice

½ teaspoon Worcestershire sauce

½ teaspoon ground black pepper

¼ teaspoon salt

¼ teaspoon garlic powder

Put all of the ingredients in a small mixing bowl and whisk until well combined.

Make Ahead

Can be made up to 2 days ahead. Store in an airtight container in the refrigerator.

	NET CARBS 0.6g			
calories	fat	protein	carbs	fiber
182	19.4g	3.7g	0.6g	0.1g

Buffalo Sauce

yield about 1½ cups (¼ cup per serving) • *prep time* 5 minutes • *cook time* 5 minutes

½ cup (1 stick) salted butter

1 cup hot sauce, at room temperature

Ground black pepper

Melt the butter in a small saucepan over medium-low heat. Pour in the hot sauce and stir continuously until the butter and hot sauce are thoroughly combined. Season with pepper to taste. Remove from the heat and allow to cool for 10 minutes before serving.

Note

When making this recipe, it's important to use room-temperature hot sauce so the ingredients blend well. A medium-hot hot sauce, such as Frank's RedHot, is ideal. Whenever a recipe in this book calls for Buffalo sauce, you can use this homemade version instead of store-bought.

Make Ahead

Can be made up to 1 week ahead. Allow to cool completely before storing in an airtight jar in the refrigerator. Stir before using.

	NET CARBS 0g			
calories	fat	protein	carbs	fiber
136	15.3g	0.2g	0g	0g

BBQ Sauce

yield about 2 cups (¼ cup per serving) • *prep time* 5 minutes • *cook time* 20 minutes

1 cup tomato paste

1 cup water

½ cup granular sweetener

⅓ cup apple cider vinegar

2 tablespoons Worcestershire sauce

2 teaspoons chili powder

1 teaspoon smoked paprika

½ teaspoon garlic powder

½ teaspoon ground cinnamon

½ teaspoon salt

Place all of the ingredients in a medium-size saucepan. Bring to a simmer over medium heat, stirring occasionally. Continue to cook at a simmer for 10 to 15 minutes, until the sauce starts to thicken. Remove from the heat and allow to cool before serving.

Note

If you don't care for the taste of bourbon, you can use this sauce in place of the bourbon BBQ sauce for the ribs on page 234.

Make Ahead

Can be made up to 5 days ahead. Allow to cool completely before storing in an airtight jar in the refrigerator. Stir before using.

	NET CARBS 3g			
calories	fat	protein	carbs	fiber
30	0.1g	1.5g	5.4g	2.4g

Multi-Purpose Dough

yield enough dough for 1 batch of pretzel bites or 1 medium pizza • *prep time* 20 minutes

2 cups finely shredded mozzarella cheese

2 ounces cream cheese (¼ cup)

1 tablespoon salted butter

¾ cup finely ground blanched almond flour

2 tablespoons coconut flour

1 large egg, whisked

2 teaspoons baking powder

1. Place the mozzarella, cream cheese, and butter in a large microwave-safe mixing bowl. Microwave on high for 90 seconds, stirring every 30 seconds. Remove from the microwave and stir until melted and smooth.

2. Add the flours, egg, and baking powder to the cheese mixture and stir with a rubber spatula to combine. Microwave on high for 10 seconds and stir again. Then mix the ingredients until they're completely combined and a firm dough comes together.

3. Roll the dough into a ball. You can use it immediately as directed in the recipe you're making or store it in the refrigerator, double-wrapped in plastic wrap, until ready to use.

Make Ahead

Can be made up to 2 days ahead. Store double-wrapped in plastic wrap in the refrigerator. When ready to use the dough, remove it from the refrigerator and allow it to sit on the counter for 15 minutes.

	NET CARBS 1.2g			
calories	fat	protein	carbs	fiber
100	8.2g	5.5g	1.9g	0.7g

Special Thanks

Many thanks to my publishing team at Victory Belt. After working with them for over six years, I'm convinced they are the best! To my editors, Pam and Holly, I could not do this without you. I've learned so much from both of you, and for that I'm sincerely grateful. To Lance and Susan, thank you for always believing in me. Your positivity helps keep me going! To Justin, Kat, and the entire design team, thank you for making *Let's Celebrate* beautiful. I appreciate how you always go the extra mile to make sure the design is just what I envisioned! I'm thankful for everyone else at Victory Belt who has worked behind the scenes to make this book possible.

To my husband, thank you for over 27 years of constant encouragement and support. In these years I've spent writing books, you've contributed to this dream in so many ways that do not go unnoticed. Thank you for helping with the extra dirty dishes and taste-testing recipes until they are perfected. Thank you for always being a shoulder to lean on or cry on. I love you, and I'm looking forward our next chapter doing life together!

To my daughter and son, I love you, and I'm so proud to be your mom. It has been an honor to watch you grow into the wonderful young adults you are, with your own careers and chasing your dreams! Thank you for supporting me in my cookbook writing endeavors over the past few years. I could not have done it without your support!

To my wonderful parents, I've been blessed with the best! Thank you for always being ready and willing to help in any way you can, from taking care of the grand-pups to testing my recipes and giving me feedback. I love you both dearly.

To my family and best friends who support me endlessly, you know who you are. I'm so blessed to have you in my life!

Resources

Measurement and Cooking Conversion Tables

LIQUIDS

¼ teaspoon	1.25 ml
½ teaspoon	2.5 ml
1 teaspoon	5 ml
1 tablespoon	15 ml
¼ cup	60 ml
⅓ cup	80 ml
½ cup	125 ml
1 cup	250 ml

DRY INGREDIENTS

1 oz	28 g
2 oz	55 g
3 oz	85 g
4 oz	115 g
8 oz	225 g
12 oz	340 g
16 oz / 1 pound	455 g
32 oz	907 g

TEMPERATURE

275°F	140°C
300°F	150°C
325°F	170°C
350°F	180°C
375°F	190°C
400°F	200°C
425°F	220°C
450°F	230°C

Brands and Products

These are some of my favorite low-carb and keto brands that make consistently tasty and high-quality products.

ChocZero

choczero.com

ChocZero makes delicious keto-friendly chocolates, syrups, and more in a wide variety of flavors. I use their sugar-free maple syrup in my recipes.

Cooks Venture

cooksventure.com

This pasture-raised heritage chicken and meat company is on a mission to build a better food system. They take care of their land with regenerative farming methods that lead to nutrient-rich soil and healthier, tastier meats.

Good Dee's

gooddees.com

Good Dee's delicious variety of mixes for cookies, cakes, crackers, and more makes low-carb and gluten-free baking a breeze. Be on the lookout, as they are always releasing new products. Their sugar-free sprinkles are another favorite of mine. Also available on Amazon.com.

Kawaii Treats and Eats

kawaiitreatsandeats.com

This brand sells delicious gluten-free, sugar-free, and keto-friendly baking mixes made with ingredients you can feel good about. Kawaii pancakes are especially yummy!

Lily's

lilyssweets.com

Lily's stevia-sweetened chocolate chips are great for baking and come in a variety of flavors. I also enjoy their chocolate bars for a sweet treat! You can find Lily's at most grocery stores and on Amazon.com.

Luv Ice Cream

This shop in St. Paul, Minnesota, sells wonderful keto ice cream and homemade baked goods. They even make their own chocolate in house! You can purchase a variety of their chocolates and baking supplies on their website, Luvicecream.net. Some of their products can also be found on amazon.com.

Whole Earth

wholeearthbrands.com

Whole Earth makes a variety of delicious plant-based sweeteners, including monk fruit, stevia, allulose, and erythritol. They come in granular and powdered varieties. They are available at Amazon.com, Costco, and most grocery stores.

These are some of my favorite low-carb and keto products.

Keto ice cream
Halo Top, Rebel, Enlighten

Low-carb bread
Lewis, Sola

Low-carb crackers
HighKey, Fat Snax, Aldi brand

Low-carb tortilla chips
Quest, Hilo, Atkins

Low-carb tortillas
Mission, La Banderita

Low-sugar marinara sauce
Mezzetta, Rao's, Victoria

Books

If you'd like to learn more about a low-carb and keto lifestyle, these are a few of the books I'd recommend. My first two books, *Southern Keto* and *Southern Keto: Beyond the Basics*, also contain useful "getting started" information, food lists, and encouragement.

- *The Art and Science of Low Carbohydrate Living* by Jeff S. Volek, PhD, RD, and Stephen D. Phinney, MD, PhD
- *The Case Against Sugar* by Gary Taubes
- *End Your Carb Confusion* by Eric C. Westman, MD, with Amy Berger, CNS
- *Keto* by Maria Emmerich and Craig Emmerich
- *Simply Keto* by Suzanne Ryan

Free Printables

On my website, ketoislife.com, you can download a PDF containing the party planning checklist from page 12, the potluck sign-up sheet from page 23, and the grocery list from page 46 so that you can print them out as needed for future party planning and shopping.

Recipe	Page	🍼	⬭	🌰	🥜	⏱
Antipasto Skewers	158	♦				♦
Everything Bagel Pigs in a Blanket	160	♦				
Jalapeño Corn Dog Poppers	162	♦	♦	♦		
Personal Charcuterie Boards	164	♦		♦		♦
Veggie Pizza	166	♦	♦	♦		
Kettle Corn	168					♦
Slow Cooker Party Meatballs	170	♦	♦			
Baked Ham & Cheese Sliders	172	♦	♦	♦		
Dill Pickle Dip	174	♦	♦			♦
Creamy Dill Pickle Chopped Salad	178	♦	♦	♦		♦
BLT Chicken Salad	180		♦			♦
Zucchini Caprese Salad	182	♦				♦
Buffalo Cobb Salad	184	♦	♦			
Blueberry & Feta Arugula Salad	186	♦		♦		♦
Hearty Spaghetti Salad	188	♦				♦
Shrimp Salad	190		♦			♦
Greek Salad	192	♦				♦
Egg Roll Soup	194					
Slow Cooker Chili for a Crowd	196					
Creamy Tuscan Chicken Soup	198	♦				
Lasagna Soup	200	♦				
Sausage Corn Chowder	202	♦				
Blender Gazpacho	204					♦
Crab & Shrimp Étouffée	208	♦		♦		
Pecan-Crusted Salmon	210			♦		♦
Asian-Inspired Beef Cups	212				♦	
Cajun Shrimp Alfredo	214	♦				
Roasted Rosemary Chicken Thighs & Radishes	216	♦				
Parmesan Garlic Wings	218	♦				
Cheesy Chicken & Rice	220	♦				
Loaded Ranch Pork Chops	222	♦	♦			
Maple & Brown Sugar–Glazed Spiral Ham	224	♦				
Sesame Chicken	226	♦	♦			
Walking Taco Bar	228	♦				
Bacon-Wrapped Stuffed Pork Tenderloin	230	♦	♦			
Slow Cooker Chipotle Shredded Beef	232					
Bourbon BBQ Ribs	234					
Hawaiian Pull-Apart Rolls	238	♦	♦	♦		
Cilantro Lime Coleslaw	240	♦	♦			♦
Roasted Garlic & Herb Breadsticks	242	♦	♦			
Creamy Cucumber Salad	244	♦				♦
Bacon Ranch Fauxtato Salad	246	♦	♦			
Okra Fritters	248	♦	♦	♦		
Mexican Cauli-Rice	250	♦				
Loaded Roasted Radishes	252	♦				
Maple Bourbon Brussels Sprouts	254					
Green Bean Casserole with Fried Onions	256	♦	♦	♦		
Roasted Veggie Skewers	258					
Lemon Ricotta Cookies	262	♦	♦	♦		♦
Cake Pops	264	♦	♦	♦		

Recipe	Page	🍼	🥑	🌰	🥜	⏱
No-Bake Cheesecake Cups	266	♦				♦
Tiramisu Mousse	268	♦				♦
Dad's Strawberry Fluff Salad	270	♦				♦
Creamy Vanilla Yogurt Fruit Dip	272	♦				♦
Chocolate Cream Cheese Dip	274	♦				♦
Strawberry Cobbler	276	♦		♦		
Double Chocolate Bundt Cake	278	♦	♦	♦		
Better-Than-Anything Cake	280	♦	♦	♦		
Turtle Pie	282	♦		♦		
Pecan Pumpkin Crisp	284	♦	♦	♦		
Strawberry Shortcake Trifle	286	♦	♦	♦		
Birthday Cake Granola	288	♦	♦	♦		
Vanilla Ice Cream	290	♦		♦		♦
Caramel Sauce	292	♦				♦
Hot Fudge Sauce	294	♦				♦
Whipped Cream	296	♦				♦
Taco Seasoning	300					♦
Ranch Seasoning	301					♦
Ranch Dressing	302	♦	♦			♦
Blue Cheese Dressing	303	♦	♦			♦
Buffalo Sauce	304	♦				♦
BBQ Sauce	305					♦
Multi-Purpose Dough	306	♦	♦	♦		♦

Recipe Index

Drinks

66
Shaken
Margarita

68
Frozen Peach
Bellini

70
Reduced-Sugar
Mimosa

72
Nonalcoholic
Party Punch

74
Blackberry
Mint Julep

76
Champagne
Punch

78
Mocha Punch

80
Bloody Mary
Bar

82
Mulled Wine

84
Hot Cocoa
for a Crowd

86
Piña Colada

88
Bubbly Sangria

90
Arnold Palmer

Quiche Lorraine—Two Ways

Bacon Cheddar Muffins

Breakfast Enchiladas

Brunch Parfaits

Home Fries

Andouille Sausage Sheet Pan Breakfast

Sheet Pan Buttermilk Pancakes

Pecan Pie Muffins

Glazed Cinnamon Biscuits

Appetizers & Bites

Nashville Hot Peanuts

Crab Rangoon-Stuffed Mushrooms

Baked Jalapeño Pimento Cheese Dip

Caramelized Onion Dip

Crispy Crackers

Shrimp Cocktail Cups

Caesar Salad Parfaits

Mini Salami Cheese Balls

Savory Party Snack Mix

Blender Salsa

Creamy Spicy Corn Dip

Restaurant-Style Queso Dip

Fiesta Layered Dip Cups

Cheesy Hot Crab Dip

Large Batch Guacamole

Pretzel Bites & Cheese Sauce

Praline Pecan Brie

Jalapeño Popper Cheese Ball

150 Pepperoni Pizza Bites

152 Bacon Jalapeño Deviled Eggs

154 Olive Pinwheels

156 Smoked Salmon Bites with Dill Cream Cheese

158 Antipasto Skewers

160 Everything Bagel Pigs in a Blanket

162 Jalapeño Corn Dog Poppers

164 Personal Charcuterie Boards

166 Veggie Pizza

168 Kettle Corn

170 Slow Cooker Party Meatballs

172 Baked Ham & Cheese Sliders

174 Dill Pickle Dip

Soups & Salads

178 Creamy Dill Pickle Chopped Salad

180 BLT Chicken Salad

182 Zucchini Caprese Salad

184 Buffalo Cobb Salad

186 Blueberry & Feta Arugula Salad

188 Hearty Spaghetti Salad

190 Shrimp Salad

192 Greek Salad

194 Egg Roll Soup

196 Slow Cooker Chili for a Crowd

198 Creamy Tuscan Chicken Soup

200 Lasagna Soup

Sausage
Corn Chowder

Blender
Gazpacho

Mains

Crab & Shrimp
Étouffée

Pecan-Crusted
Salmon

Asian-Inspired
Beef Cups

Cajun Shrimp
Alfredo

Roasted
Rosemary
Chicken Thighs
& Radishes

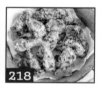
Parmesan
Garlic Wings

Cheesy
Chicken & Rice

Loaded Ranch
Pork Chops

Maple & Brown
Sugar-Glazed
Spiral Ham

Sesame
Chicken

Walking
Taco Bar

Bacon-Wrapped
Stuffed
Pork Tenderloin

Slow Cooker
Chipotle
Shredded Beef

Bourbon
BBQ Ribs

Sides

238
Hawaiian
Pull-Apart Rolls

240
Cilantro Lime
Coleslaw

242
Roasted
Garlic & Herb
Breadsticks

244
Creamy
Cucumber
Salad

246
Bacon Ranch
Fauxtato Salad

248
Okra Fritters

250
Mexican
Cauli-Rice

252
Loaded Roasted
Radishes

254
Maple Bourbon
Brussels
Sprouts

256
Green Bean
Casserole with
Fried Onions

258
Roasted Veggie
Skewers

Desserts

262
Lemon Ricotta
Cookies

264
Cake Pops

266
No-Bake
Cheesecake
Cups

268
Tiramisu
Mousse

270
Dad's
Strawberry Fluff
Salad

272
Creamy Vanilla
Yogurt Fruit Dip

274
Chocolate
Cream Cheese
Dip

276
Strawberry
Cobbler

278
Double
Chocolate
Bundt Cake

280
Better-Than-
Anything Cake

282
Turtle Pie

284
Pecan Pumpkin
Crisp

286
Strawberry
Shortcake Trifle

288
Birthday Cake
Granola

290
Vanilla
Ice Cream

292
Caramel Sauce

294
Hot Fudge
Sauce

296
Whipped
Cream

Basics

300
Taco Seasoning

301
Ranch Seasoning

302
Ranch Dressing

303
Blue Cheese Dressing

304
Buffalo Sauce

305
BBQ Sauce

306
Multi-Purpose Dough

General Index